Overcoming Obstacles

Experiences of Black Financial Services Professionals

by

Dr. C.W. Copeland, ChFC®, CLU®, RICP®

Dr. James M. Moten Jr., CFP®, ChFC®, AFC®

Dr. Crystal Hudson

LaTossha-Monique Joseph, MS

Table of Contents Page

Introduction

This book is a collection of interviews of successful Black Financial Services Professionals. Their stories were necessitated by comments frequently made about the availability of intellectual talent in the Black financial services community.

A recent article in a popular financial magazine showed a picture of a diverse group of Americans and posed the question "which of these is a financial advisor?". Unfortunately, the vast majority of respondents identified a white male in his late 50's. If this is the prototypical advisor, what is the future of the Black financial services professional? If this is the prototypical advisor, what is the wealth effect on their families for generations?

In over 20 years of practice, we have observed Black financial services professionals enter and leave the business, not because of lack of desire, or lack of skills, but for lack of viable clients. While sales are a "numbers game", access to viable clients is too and when the numbers are skewed against you due to "selectivity", the probability of success lessens considerably. Selectivity seems to happen more when the services provided are professional in nature. Unofficial data suggests that consumers choose professional services from people who look like them or whom they assume is competent.

The advisors interviewed in this book have demonstrated their ability to achieve against the odds and have demonstrated perseverance to transcend longevity constraints. Their stories will inspire other Black financial services professionals, but more so generate more conversations about why Black financial services professionals are viable options as advisors.

A by-product of this project is the potential for mentoring of aspiring professionals who have chosen this not only as a career, but as a degreed field. There are over 400 CFP Board Registered Programs in the U.S., with only a handful established at HBCUs. We highlight the Program established at Clark-Atlanta University as a model for development.

About the authors

C. W. Copeland, Ph.D., ChFC®, CLU®, RICP®

C. W. Copeland, Ph.D. is the President of the Financial Planning Division of the National Financial Group. Dr. Copeland is also an Adjunct Professor at **The American College of Financial Services,** an Adjunct Professor at the **College for Financial Planning** and an Adjunct Professor at **Clark-Atlanta University**. Dr. Copeland holds a Ph.D. in Financial Planning and conducts scholarly research in Behavioral Economics and teaches graduate-level business courses. He has been a regular guest on radio and television shows across the country where he addresses audiences on financial planning strategies on a regular basis.

Dr. Copeland has authored/edited several textbooks to include *Financial Services Overview: The Practicum,* editor of *McGill's Life Insurance,* co-author of *Applications in Financial Planning I & II,* co-editor of *Essentials of Life Insurance Products,* and co-editor of *Essentials of Disability Income Insurance,* all published by The American College of Financial Services. Dr. Copeland also co-wrote "Chapter 17: Insurance and Risk Management" for Victor Ricciardi's book *Financial Behavior: Players, Services, Products, and Markets,* published by Oxford Press. He is also the co-author of The Personal Economic Model, published by Alliance Publishing.

Dr. Copeland has served for 22 years as an instructor with R.S. Thomas Training Associates providing pre-licensing training, continuing education, and business development advice for financial services professionals. Dr. Copeland has nearly 25 years of industry experience as a financial planner where he coordinates the efforts of attorneys, tax advisors, employee benefits coordinators, estate and business planners, and pension managers for the benefit of his clients. He holds numerous licenses and registrations (in multiple states) in the areas of investments and insurance and holds the prestigious Chartered Financial Consultant (ChFC®) and Chartered Life Underwriter (CLU®) designations.

James M. Moten Jr., PhD, MSFP, CFP®, ChFC®, AFC®, CRPC®, CMFC®

Dr. James M. Moten Jr., is the Program Director and Assistant Professor for the Masters of Science of Financial Planning Program at The American College of Financial Services. Additionally, he is the Vice President of the Financial Planning Division of the National Financial Group. He is a former Personal Financial Counselor for Zeiders Enterprises and Advisor and Registered Representative for Primerica Finance Services.

Dr. Moten has a PhD in Business Administration (Financial Management Concentration), a Master of Science in Finance, a Master of Science in Accounting, a Master of Science Economics, a Master of Business Administration, a Master of Science in Financial Planning and a Master of Science in Acquisition and Contract Management. In addition to his academic degree's, he holds the Series 7, Series 6, Series 65, Series 63, Series 26, Life and Health, and Property and

Casualty Licenses in multiple states. Lastly, he holds the Certified Financial Planner CFP®, Chartered Financial Consultant ChFC®, Accredited Financial Counselor AFC®, Chartered Mutual Fund Counselor CMFC®, and Chartered Retirement Planning Counselor CRPC® professional designations.

Dr. Moten Co-Authored Financial Planning for Poor People: Financial Professionals Guide to Working with Low-Income to Middle-Income Individuals. In addition, Dr. Moten has published three textbooks: *Advanced Financial Management: Theory and Application*; *Introductory Financial Management: Theory and Application*; and *Personal Financial Literacy: A Practical Approach* through BVT Publishing. Dr. Moten also co-wrote "Chapter 17: Insurance and Risk Management" for Victor Ricciardi's book *Financial Behavior: Players, Services, Products, and Markets*, published by Oxford Press.

Dr. Crystal R. Hudson

Dr. Crystal R. Hudson is currently the Chair of the Accounting and Finance Department in the School of Business at Clark-Atlanta University (CAU). Also, since its inception, Dr. Crystal R. Hudson has served as the Director of CAU's Financial Planning program, a program that produces future Certified Financial Planners (CFPs). Dr. Hudson has a stellar research record focusing on the economic lives of African Americans.

Prior to coming to CAU, Dr. Hudson had a successful career in Corporate Finance with such companies as The Weather Channel, Haagen Dazs and Sara Lee, Inc.

Dr. Hudson earned a B. S. in Operations & Systems Management from Indiana University, MBA in Finance from Clark Atlanta University, and Ph. D. in Financial Planning and Consumer Economics from the University of Georgia.

LaTossha-Monique Joseph, M.S.

LaTossha-Monique Joseph received two B.S degrees in finance, and risk management from the California State University of Sacramento, and the M.S. degree in finance from Kaplan University in 2006, and 2016, respectively. Since 2017, she has been with Primerica Financial Services, where she is currently a Financial Coach.

ISBN: 978-1-7368119-3-1

Bowker Publishing

Published: June 21, 2021

Finance Careers

Finance careers focus on three primary areas: financial services, finance related and corporate finance. There may be features that are similar in each area, but the distinction calls for three separate areas. In theory, financial services jobs have a direct relationship with cash, or cash equivalents such as banking, stock broker and financial planning. Finance related occupations include insurance agents and real estate agents and the corporate finance area explores the role of the cash manager, credit analyst and financial manager.

Finance Certifications and Licensure

There are many licenses and certifications that can be earned for financial services or financial analysts' careers. However, there are a few certifications that are considered more important in the area of comprehensive financial planning. The Certified Financial Planner Certification CFP®, Chartered Financial Consultant ChFC® are the two most recognized certification in this area. The Certified Financial Analyst CFA® is the most widely known certification of financial analyst. The CFP® is issued by the Certified Financial Planner Board of Standards Incorporated. There are 8 principal topic areas which make up the CFP® curriculum. The 8 principal topic areas include:
A. Professional Conduct and Regulation
B. General Principles of Financial Planning
C. Education Planning
D. Risk Management and Insurance Planning,
E. Investment Planning
F. Tax Planning
G. Retirement Savings and Income Planning
H. Estate Planning

In addition to passing a 6-hour, 170 question computer-based CFP® certification exam and taking seven financial planning courses; an individual must possess a bachelor's degree or higher and have at least three years of full-time personal financial planning experience. The ChFC® is issued by the American College of Financial Services. Candidates must complete nine required courses to include their corresponding exams and three years of full-time business experience. The CFA® Institute issues the CFA®. In addition to passing three exams; an individual must possess an undergraduate degree and have four years of professional experience. Many financial service professionals get their start in the insurance industry. In order to stand apart many of them also pursue designations. The Chartered Life Underwriter CLU® provides in-depth knowledge of life insurance concepts and life insurance law within the context of overall risk management; the necessary knowledge to help clients address their estate planning needs; and an understanding of solutions addressing the life insurance needs of business owners and professionals. Financial planners also specialize in areas such as retirement planning. These individuals have to opportunity to pursue the Retirement Income Certified Professional RICP®

Across the financial services landscape, in addition to holding a designation, there is usually a licensure requirement. The Series 7 - General Securities Representative Exam (Stockbroker), Series 6 - Investment Company and Variable Contracts Exam (Mutual Funds/Variable Annuities) Series 63 - Uniform Securities Agent State Law Exam Series 65 - Uniform Registered Investment Adviser Law Exam (RIA), Series 66 - Uniform Investment Adviser - Combined State Laws Exam (Combined 63 and 65) and the Series 79 - Investment Banking Exam are the most common. The licenses require intense study and the exams are administered at an approved testing site. Securities firms in the U.S are regulated by the Financial Industry Regulatory

Authority (FINRA). FINRA is the largest self-regulatory organization (SRO) in the securities industry in the United States. An SRO is a membership-based organization that creates and enforces rules for members based on the federal securities laws. SROs, which are overseen by the Securities and Exchange Commission (SEC), are the front line in regulating broker-dealers. The Securities and Exchange Commission (SEC) is a government commission created by Congress to regulate the securities markets and protect investors. In addition to regulation and protection, it also monitors the corporate takeovers in the U.S. The SEC is composed of five commissioners appointed by the U.S. President and approved by the Senate. The statutes administered by the SEC are designed to promote full public disclosure and to protect the investing public against fraudulent and manipulative practices in the securities markets. An applicant must currently be working for a member firm in order to sit for most securities examinations. Prior to receiving approval to sit for an exam a background check must be conducted to ensure the individual seeking licensure has not committed any financial industry related crime.

The Lack of Diversity in Financial Services

Services provided by the financial services industry assist families in building wealth which promotes overall economic growth. The agents who are client facing must relate to their clients and earn the trust of those clients. Although, the minority population will be the majority population by 2045 (African Americans make up 13.3 percent and Hispanic Americans make up 17.8 percent of the U.S population) there is a distinct disparity in the financial services industry according to ethnicity. The financial services profession is an agent driven field. The United States Government Accountability Office (GAO) conducted a survey to find out how diverse senior management is in the industry. Their 2018 study found that Black or African Americans males comprised 2 percent while African American women comprised 1 percent, Hispanic American males comprised 2 percent and Hispanic American women comprised 1 percent, Asian American men comprised 4 percent while Asian American women comprised 2 percent. All other minority groups made up less than 1 percent. Caucasian American Males comprised 60 percent while Caucasian women comprised 26 percent of the industry. There are over 85,000 Certified Financial Planners and African American and Hispanic American combined make up only 3.7 percent of these professionals. This book surveyed Eleven successful African American financial services professionals to ascertain the hurdles they faced and still face in the financial services industry. This book could provide information on how to remove some of the tangible and intangible barriers to entry in this robust industry. The authors of this book have worked or currently work in the financial services industry in some capacity. They have all faced their own set of obstacles and sought out to find if they were alone in this journey.

Advanced Education in Financial Planning

When a financial planner wants an advanced level of education, they can pursue a MS in Financial Planning. There are a few institutions that specialize in this type of degree. The most prestigious institutions in this area includes The American College of Financial Services, Kansas State University, Texas Tech University, University of Georgia and the University of Missouri. Below is the Master of Science in Financial Planning Program at the American College of Financial Services with two of its concentrations. The concentration not shown is the retirement planning concentration. The Master of Science in Financial Planning (MSFP) at the American College of Financial Services is an innovative and unique program. It prepares students for successful careers as a financial planner, financial counselor, retirement specialist and investment advisors with advanced knowledge in tax, estate, risk management, behavioral finance, asset protection and investment management. Students will learn financial planning principles using sound, ethical, business practices. Graduates of the Advance Financial Planning concentration are prepared to sit for the CFP® examination through a rigorous curriculum and in-depth course content. Graduates of the

Master of Science in Financial Planning (30 credits)
Core Courses
MSFP 531 Family Financial Planning
MSFP 569 Legacy Planning Reimagined
MSFP 571 Behavioral Finance for Financial Planners
MSFP 630 Advanced Case Studies and Application **(Capstone)**
Advanced Financial Planning Concentration
MSFP 534 Personal Income Taxation and Decision Making
MSFP 537 Retirement Planning and Employee Benefits
MSFP 538 Investment Theory and Portfolio Management
MSFP 539 Estate Management and Planned Giving
MSFP 551 Insurance Analysis for Families
MSFP 633 Personal Financial Planning Case Study
Retirement Planning Concentration
MSFP 615 Advanced Estate Management and Planned Giving
MSFP 543 Business Succession Strategies
MSFP 553 Retirement Income Process, Strategies & Solutions
MSFP 554 Sources of Retirement Income
MSFP 555 Managing the Retirement Income Plan
MSFP 631 Advanced Retirement Planning Issues
Legacy Planning Concentration
MSFP 543 Business Succession Strategies
MSFP 544 Planning for Impact in the Context of Family Wealth

MSFP 549 Charitable Giving Strategies
MSFP 559 Gift Planning in a Nonprofit Context
MSFP 534 Personal Income Taxation and Decision Making
MSFP 615 Advanced Estate Management and Planned Giving

Financial Planning Organizations

There are a few prominent financial planning organizations that have recently instituted diversity initiatives to attract more planers of color. The most notable national organizations include the Financial Planning Association **(FPA),** the National Association of Personal Financial Advisors **(NAPFA)** and the Association of African American Financial Advisors **(AAAA).** One organization in particular sets itself apart. The **ASSOCIATION OF AFRICAN AMERICAN FINANCIAL ADVISORS (AAAA)** was created to address the needs and concerns of African American Financial Professionals. AAAA is a non-profit membership organization for African American financial advisors and affiliated professionals. They work in alliance with academic leaders at Historically Black Colleges and Universities (HBCUs) that support financial planning degree programs, legislative and regulatory bodies, financial services firms and consumer interest organizations. AAAA fosters the value of financial planning and advances the financial planning profession. https://www.aaafainc.com/

The Importance of Diversity in Financial Services

"Don't put all your eggs in one basket; diversification is key". A quote I often hear throughout my career, as advice to clients seeking stronger portfolios. The irony comes when we expect financial services companies to reflect diversity within the workforce. According to the US Bureau of Labor Statistics, 82% of the financial services workforce is White; while only 6% of the workforce are comprised of Black personnel. Due to the demand of diversity and inclusion, financial companies are looking at the data. What they are discovering will bring positive changes to the financial services industry, and racial and ethnic inclusion plays a key role.

3 Ways Racial and Ethnic Diversity Strengthen the Financial Services Industry.

-Increases Productivity and Profitability

Financial service CEO's experience growing performance in profitability after incorporating more racial and ethnic diversity into their company's workforce culture. According to the 2019 McKinsey & Co Study (2020), companies ranking in the top quartile, with racial and ethnic inclusive diversity practices, outperformed competitors by 36% in terms of profitability. Embracing diversity shows personnel how valued they are. This increases productivity, which adds extreme value to any industry. Racial and ethnic inclusion not only enhances performance and profitability, but also gives spark to that creativity and innovation that only comes from the uniqueness of differences.

-Fresh Innovations Maximize Competitive Edge

A group of fresh eyes, with different life experiences solve old problems in new and creative ways. Herring (2009) suggest that innovation depend less on lone thinkers with high intelligence then on diverse groups working together and capitalizing on their individuality. Companies are quickly realizing that diverse group collaboration inspire creative juices, in the form of new ideas. Diversity gives a voice to underrepresented groups within the financial services industry, which includes them in the mastermind process. Proper representation is what the next generation of workforce/wealth builders are demanding.

-Proper Representation and Brand Loyalty

Brand loyalty is a big motivator for financial services companies, encouraging them to adapt to the new diversity and inclusion recommendations. According to Pew Research Center, millennials have surpassed Baby Boomers making up 35% of Americans in the labor force. All this influence leaks over to client retention as well. According to a Harvard Business review, a team with a member who shares a client's ethnicity is 152% likelier than another team to understand that client. Financial service CEOs see the benefits in proper representation of racial and ethnic groups. They know that generational wealth transfers will be passed to companies that promote diversity and inclusion. The financial service companies that embrace these diversity demands are the leaders of a strong new financial services industry.

Increased racial and ethnic diversity and awareness in financial services is dynamically strengthening the industry. These benefits are well documented and experienced by financial company CEOs, and their personnel as well. The more financial service companies embrace a more diverse working environment, performance and profitability increase, and innovation and loyalty will expand. These benefits to the industry, and within company culture, is directly correlated to the respect and gratitude workers feel from being properly represented. Therefore; diversity brings stability to the financial industry; just as it does to an investment portfolio.

HBCU Focus: Clark Atlanta University Financial Planning Program

Clark Atlanta University is a Registered Program with the CFP Board of Standards, which is the licensing body for Certified Financial Planners. In essence, CAU's Financial Planning Program educates future Certified Financial Planners. CAU's Financial Planning Program started in 2014 through a collaboration with the University of Georgia's Financial Planning program. I along with my major professor, CAU's current School of Business Dean, and a prominent CFP in the Atlanta area collaborated to start CAU's Financial Planning program.

We initially formed a Board for CAU's Financial Planning program, and I have served as the Director of CAU's Financial Planning Program since its inception in 2014. The School of Business has always taught a Personal Finance course as an elective and on average there were 15 to 20 students, per semester, in that course. We revamped this course and turned it into the first course of the Financial Planning program. It reviews each personal finance area such as retirement, estate planning, insurance, tax, and investments. This course also covers the CFP industry, CFP careers including ethics and Code of Standards.

Within the finance department of the School of Business, finance students can obtain a Dual Concentration in Finance and Financial Planning and students outside of finance and outside the School of Business can geta a Financial Planning minor. With a dual degree in finance and financial planning, finance students have the flexibility of pursuing a career in financial services or a career in corporate finance. Also, students within the Atlanta University Center (AUC), which are Clark Atlanta University,

Spelman College and Morehouse College, have the option of taking courses on each other's campuses. So, students from Morehouse College and Spelman College can receive a major from their home school and a minor in Financial Planning from CAU.

From the inception of CAU's Financial Planning Program, I've always formed partnerships with Corporations to expose students to the CFP industry and professionals to provide them with mentors and experience through internships and full-time positions. Executives from these partnerships served as board members for CAU's Financial Planning program. Inauguration Partnerships were formed with Apex Financial, Morgan Stanley and Ally Financial.

Results from CAU's Financial Planning Program

In 2018, the School of Business and several schools within the university decided to make the first Personal Finance course one of three required courses for its freshman to increase their financial literacy. As a result, the finance department, within the School of Business, now teaching approx. 600 students per year as opposed to approx. 50 per year; which gave CAU's Financial Planning program more exposure through these classes.

The success of CAU's Financial Planning program is in its graduates. After only seven short years, these graduates have infiltrated the Financial Services Industry. The majority of students within the program are finance students who pursed a Dual Concentration in Finance and Financial Planning and they have gone on to work within the financial services industry for Morgan Stanley, Merrill Lynch, TIAA, AlphaSights, the FDIC (Federal Deposit Insurance Corporation), FINRA (Financial Industry Regulatory Authority), Ally Financial, Caterpillar Financial, PNC Bank and many more. Outside of finance, many students major in accounting and minor in Financial Planning so they can pursue a CPA and a CFP. We have also had several Morehouse students receive their finance degree from Morehouse and receive a minor from Clark Atlanta University, by taking CAU's six financial planning courses.

Standouts include a graduate who recently obtained his CFP and is now an Assistant Vice President & Financial Solutions Advisor for Merrill Lynch. Prior to this, he had a Farmers Insurance Agency. Another standout graduate recently started with FINRA (Financial Industry Regulatory Authority) as a Senior Compliance professional. Prior to this he excelled with TIAA in the investment and compliance area. Another graduate took a slightly different route and worked for the Federal Deposit Insurance Corporation (FDIC) evaluating the solvency of banks within the Southeast region. Now she works as a consultant for Price Waterhouse Coopers Company. Finally, one standout who graduated just prior to the Financial Planning program becoming official but he took most of the financial planning courses. Out of CAU he went to work for Wells Fargo as an Advisor within their Wealth Management division. He worked his way up through their Capital Markets division and is now a Strategic Consultant – Middle Market Investment Banking at Wells Fargo.

Reuben Lewis

Professional Biography

Reuben Lewis IV is a results-driven and client focused financial services professional with 22 years of value adding contributions. Reuben is known as an influential leader with a special talent for building both cooperative and productive working relationships with clients, team members, and insurance carriers. Reuben's areas of strength are:

1. Team Building

2. Recruiting

3. Insurance Planning & Personal Risk Management

4. Retirement Planning

5. Investment Portfolio Analysis

6. Long Term Care Insurance Planning

7. Financial Planning & Estate Planning

Reuben developed a passion for retirement planning and investment portfolio analysis while serving as a Retirement Specialist for Nationwide Retirement Solutions. While serving in this role, Reuben was responsible for managing municipal 457b retirement plans totaling more than $200 million in assets. Reuben later developed his skill sets of team building, recruiting, insurance planning, and personal risk management while serving as a Nationwide Insurance agency owner. During his tenure as an agency owner, his agency was consistently recognized as one of the top 10 agencies in Georgia for multi-line production. Reuben built a multi-line operation of 11 Nationwide Insurance store fronts with 60 employees. Reuben also served on the Nationwide Agent Advisory council during his time as an agency owner. Reuben demonstrated his expertise in long term care insurance planning by working with several major credit unions in Georgia to offer long term care planning to members.

Currently, Reuben utilizes his skills and passion for the industry in as President of National Financial Group. In this position, Reuben offers strategic leadership by sourcing, recruiting and mentoring new representatives which allows him to build his team while helping others grow as entrepreneurs, as well as complete oversight and vision for the development of the firm. As a financial planner, Reuben is able to further his belief in holistic financial analysis and has made financial planning the top focus for the firm.

Social Media links www.nfgo.com

Why did you choose this field?

Since a young age, I have always been curious about the financial markets and how they work in relationship to the products and services provided to consumers within those markets. This prompted me to start pursuing a career in financial services as teenager, where at the age of 18, I obtained my temporary life insurance license with the state of Georgia and pursued a career with Primerica as a financial representative. While doing this, I learned the basics of financial markets, products and services. As I learned more and more in this role, I became more passionate about financial services, which led me to want a more formal education to become more knowledgeable in this field. I chose to pursue a degree in Finance with a concentration in Risk Management and Insurance, and graduated in 2000 from a great institution of higher learning, Georgia Southern University.

While pursing my degree in finance, I had a chance to take the Financial Markets & Investments course from Dr. John Hatem. That course further inspired me to know at some point in my career I wanted to start my own financial planning firm so I could make a profound impact on the lives of people in my community by empowering them to be financially independent through financial literacy and education. One other important take away I gained from the class is you always have to have an insatiable appetite for learning if you are going to keep up with the ever-changing financial services industry.

The second factor that motived me to start my own firm, and as founder of National Financial Group, I have seen firsthand the irreparable damage and financial devastation that can be caused from financial practitioners that do not have that insatiable appetite for learning. Unfortunately, many of the practitioners I have come across in my career that have caused this damage were CPAs. Many I have found do not have an insatiable appetite for learning, which means they do not stay abreast of the ever-changing tax code, which causes them not to be able to help their clients adequately mitigate their tax liability and build wealth. I wholeheartedly believe I want to be a part of the solution to this problem by staying committed to learning and professional excellence within the Financial Services Industry. This additional formal education will allow me to increase my knowledge and add to my unique skill set, which will allow me to effect positive change within the accounting and financial services industry.

My insatiable appetite for learning has allowed me to build National Financial Group into one of the top independently owned financial services firms in the country. This is represented by the following facts:

- Top Independent General Agency in 2019 and 2020 with Security Mutual Life of New York
- Top 10 General Agency for OneAmerica Life Insurance in 2019 and 2020
- Top 10 General Agency for Lafayette Life Insurance in 2019 and 2020

- Advisory Council member with Security Mutual Life Of New York

My goal is to continue to grow my firm by hiring a diverse group of over 100 CPAs to serve my client base in my three office locations in Scottsdale, AZ, Atlanta, GA and Miami, FL. This will subsequently allow me to continue to pursue my dream to empower my clients and help them achieve financial independence through financial literacy and education.

What experience caused you to consider leaving the field?

Dealing with sales managers that lacked talent and knowledge who were extremely negative and provided no support.

What made you stay?

I knew that I had the talent and knowledge to be very successful in this industry. So, I just focused on my belief in myself and built my own training & development program and support group of peers.

What would you consider the "standard" for our industry?

Cirilo Mc Sween (The first black life agent for New York Life)

What do you perceive the consumer sees as the "standard"?

Some white male in a suit.

Approximately what percentage of your clients are Black? Is this by choice or default?

80%. This is definitely by choice because I believe my community needs more help than any other to close the wealth gap in this country.

What roadblocks have you had acquiring clients of other races?

They are typically very untrusting and skeptical of my professional competency.

If you were not able to acquire clients of other races, what impact doyou think it would have on your overall wealth?

None.

Are Black Financial Services Professionals hindered in their pursuit ofbuilding wealth?

Yes.

If so, what are the factors that impact it?

They are not given enough opportunities to earn income within the industry. This is caused by lack of initial training & development, and followed up by restricted or no access to support and resources from the financial services firms they represent.

Is the generational wealth transfer of Black Financial Services Professionals in jeopardy due to an inability to acquire clients of otherraces?

No. This would quickly become a non-issue if a larger percentage of blacks did business exclusively with black advisors. However, if that does not happen, then "yes", this will be a major factor that limits wealth transfer of black financial services professionals.

The American College for Financial Services has a scholarship targeted towards African-Americans to increase the numbers of us inthe field. What other incentives do you think our industry can put inplace to achieve this goal?

Firms should provide tuition reimbursement programs for minority candidates. There should also be outreach programs from various financial services firms that go out and do career road shows in minority communities throughout the U.S. This would show minorities the various opportunities that are available and educate them on what they need to do to pursue those opportunities.

Were you given an opportunity to intern with a more experiencedadvisor?

No.

What advice would you give an undergraduate student who was considering financial services/planning as a career?

First find out all of the educational and licensing requirements and complete them while you are in college or early in your academic/career life cycle. Secondly, find a well accomplished industry veteran and get them to mentor you, and actually listen to and follow their advice.

Jocelyn Wright

Professional Biography

- Educational background
    - BS, Business Administration (Finance), University of Delaware
    - MBA Finance, Howard University
- Years in the industry
    - 28 years financial services
    - 19 years financial advisor/planner
- Licenses, professional certifications, or designations
    - Certified Financial Planner (CFP®)
    - Retirement Income Certified Professional (RICP®)
- Honors/Awards
    - InvestmentNews Women to Watch, 2016
    - Association of African American Financial Advisors 50 Under 50, 2020
- Social Media links
    - LinkedIn:

https://www.linkedin.com/in/jocelyndwright/
  - Twitter: @jocelyndwright
- Articles/Books/Interviews
- Family info

Why did you choose this field?

As a child growing up in the 70s, we played board games and I always wanted to be the banker. I loved counting money. Also, my father owned two cash-based businesses and on the weekends, he would let me count the money and organize the receipts. So, for a while I thought I would go into banking.

However, during my sophomore year of college my paternal grandmother passed away. It turned out she only had a $5,000 life insurance policy, likely a debit policy, that was not enough to cover her funeral expenses. Consequently, my father and his siblings had to pay for any additional expenses. It made me think how many other (Black) families are going through this same thing when a loved one dies.

It was the result of my childhood experience along with my grandmother's death and working in credit card collections during college that led to my interest in personal financial planning. It is the perfect combination of my organizational skills and interest in money.

What experience caused you to consider leaving the field? What made you stay?

I am extremely fortunate that I have not had any traumatic experiences (such as blatant racism, sexism, or other macro aggressions). However, there have been many times when I thought I had had enough, I am going to get a job, be employee of the month and get the front parking space. This usually happened when I was struggling to make the income, I thought I should, or not being at a certain level, when I did not get the big client, or when it felt like it was all too much. Thankfully, those times are behind me now. Here I am, nearly twenty years in and I feel that I am beginning to hit my stride and greater things are ahead.

What made you stay?

Reminding myself why I choose this career in the first place. My desire to help and make an impact in the profession. Certainly, my clients and my family who have supported me as well. It also helps to have at least one person, they do not necessarily have to be in this field, who will listen to you when you are having a moment and talk you off the ledge.

What would you consider the 'standard' for our industry?

First, you must remember that financial planning is still a relatively young profession unlike the legal and medical professions where there are established standards - undergraduate degree, graduate school, pass the required exam(s), etc. We do not currently have such a standard. I believe the CFP Board of Standards is working toward that to make the CFP® certification the standard for our profession. Otherwise, anyone can put up a shingle and call themselves a financial advisor/planner.

What do you perceive the consumer sees as the 'standard'?

Unfortunately, because there is no clearly defined standard it creates a tremendous amount of confusion for consumers. Without an established requirement anyone can call themselves a financial adviser. This contributes to the mistrust and misperceptions that the public has about our industry.

Approximately what percentage of your clients are Black? Is this by choice or default?

Over 90% of my clients are Black. I would say it is a combination of choice and default. My goal is to financially empower and increase the wealth in my community. It is not that I will not or do not work with clients who are not Black, I certainly will and do. My networks and social circles are primarily Black.

What types of issues have you had winning the confidence of your natural market?

I do not know if it is necessarily winning the confidence of my natural market, I feel that because working with a financial professional is not done broadly within the Black community there still exists a lack of understanding. There are different business models and confusion about how to engage a financial professional - do you need one, do you pay, how much to pay, etc.

Also, there have been times when some potential clients wanted to work with someone who was with a large, 'brand name' firm or who believed that the 'other man's' ice is colder.

Elaborate on your niche:

My niche is personal - professional Black women. When I started as a financial advisor, I noticed a gap in how the industry marketed to this segment. Professional Black women are too often overlooked and underserved, especially if you are single without children. The skill set necessary to work with this group, I would say, is the ability to listen to and understand our needs, not see us as a monolith or one size fits all. I do not believe I would take a different approach if I were to start over because there is still a gap in how Black women are marketed to and supported in our industry.

What roadblocks have you had acquiring clients of other races?

I would not necessarily say that I have had roadblocks acquiring clients of other races. Again, working in my 'natural market', I have clients largely from my community. I have not actively pursued clients of other races enough to face any.

Do you think that you are missing out by not having non-Black clients?

Given my desire to work with those who are overlooked and underserved, even if I had a larger number of non-Black clients, they would still fit in that category. So, I cannot say that I would necessarily be missing out. Furthermore, when you say missing out, what is that referring to exactly, is it simply income or is there something else?

Additionally, so much as changed since I began working with clients in 2002. Technology has a way of leveling the playing field. There are expanded ways of building your brand and impacting more individuals beyond your base of clients. You must look outside of the 'normal' way of doing things. You can absolutely be successful in working within our community.

If you were not able to acquire clients of other races, what impact do you think it would have on your overall wealth?

I am unable to answer this question given that only a small percentage of my clients are from other races.

Are Black Financial Services Professionals hindered in their pursuit of building wealth? If so, what are the factors that impact it?

If you assume that Black professionals will primarily work with Black consumers, under the 'traditional' business model and given the wealth disparities in our community we would not be as financially successful as our white counterparts. However, the profession has evolved in that there are other business models available that are not solely dependent on a client's investable assets.

Additionally, we can help advisors develop the skills and perhaps equally important, the confidence, to work with different communities and cultures. There still exists the thinking that if something is run by or features a Black person it only caters to a Black audience versus having mass appeal. We have seen in music and movies that this is not the case and I believe the same can be true in financial services.

Is the generational wealth transfer of Black Financial Services Professional in jeopardy due to an inability to acquire clients of other races?

I think the wealth transfer of Black financial services professionals is more in jeopardy due to a lack of succession planning.

As we know, succession planning is a major issue in our profession regardless of the race or ethnicity of the individual. If we fail to put plans in place and value our business, unfortunately when we pass away or retire the clients simply go away either to another advisor or are left to manage things on their own.

Too often, when we think about starting a business, we think about doing it alone. Do not get me wrong, partnering is not easy. You have to find the right one(s) and you may 'kiss a few frogs' in the process. But just as in any relationship when you do it can be a match made in heaven. It reminds me of the African Proverb, *If you want to go fast, go alone. If you want to go far, go together*. The benefit should be more than just two people coming together. You should be able to do even more together by joining forces.

The American College for Financial Services has a scholarship targeted towards African Americans to increase the numbers of us in the field. What other incentives do you think our industry can put in place to achieve this goal?

First, I do not know if I would call it incentives vs. programs. However, when you look at some of the reasons why Blacks are underrepresented in the professional, they include the cost of education and that is where scholarships like the one offered through The American College help to minimize that financial hurdle. Other programs can include the following:

- Hiring more Black faculty to teach financial planning courses
- Increasing the number of financial planning programs at Historically Black Colleges and Universities (HBCUs)
- Creating more opportunities for internships and apprenticeships
- Teaching and requiring financial education starting in elementary school
- Firms tying compensation and performance bonuses to hiring and more importantly, retention goals for Black professionals

Were you given an opportunity to intern with a more experienced advisor? If so, where, and when?

Although I have worked in financial services for nearly thirty years, I did not become a financial advisor until my early 30s. Honestly, I did not consider an internship.

How do you think an internship might have been beneficial?

An internship may have been beneficial in that it would have allowed me the opportunity to see a day in the life of a financial advisor. Additionally, I would have had an opportunity to meet other professionals and begin building my network. However, as I stated earlier, I was already committed to the profession, I knew it was something that I wanted to do, and I did not need the extra push.

What advice would you give to an undergrad student who was considering financial services/ planning as a career?

I think this is a great time to enter the profession. There are so many opportunities for young planners. As you know, there are more CFP® professionals over the age of seventy than under the age of 30. This creates tremendous opportunities for younger planners to join firms where they come in as a junior planner and can potentially take over a firm or book of business as the senior planner begins to reduce their hours and ultimately retires.

I would encourage a student to become familiar with the different business models and determine which one is right for them. Of course, keeping in mind that where they start is not where they must stay.

Find a mentor(s) as well as a sponsor. A sponsor is someone who will have a vested interest in your success. They can get you opportunities that you might not otherwise get on your own.

Get your CFP® certification in the first 1-3 years, if possible.

And if you are thinking of starting your own practice, consider partnership. But remember 1+1 should equal 3 or more!

Do you think the industry should restrict the use of titles?

No, I am not saying that at all. You should be allowed to use titles if you meet certain qualifications. Just as a doctor or attorney cannot use the title without certain qualifications, I believe the same should be true of a financial planning professional. And if we want to be recognized as a profession then that should be a goal.

If you could take a mulligan on your career, what would you do differently?

I do my best not to live in the past and have regrets because I strongly believe that things happen for a reason. Also, I do not want God (the Universe) to think that I am not grateful for my blessings. With that being said, when asked this question I usually say, if I had to do it over again, I would have had a fully funded emergency reserve of twelve months of expenses. That would have given me a peace of mind in the beginning that could have made a significant difference in my early years as an advisor.

Intentionally Left Blank

Darrell J. Williams

Professional Biography

Financial Professional, MassMutual Financial

CA Insurance License # 0620034
MassMutual Pacific
1435 River Park Drive, Suite 410
Sacramento, CA 95815

Phone **(916) 437-1710** | Fax (916) 641-0385

darrellwilliams@financialguide.com

Educational Background: AA degree Architectural/ Drafting 1981, Hayward, Ca. AA degree Biblical Studies, Capitol Bible College, Sacramento, Ca. 1999. Numerous Certificates and course completions in Business Planning, Estate Planning and Retirement Planning.

Years in the Industry; Started in 1982 Sales Management Trainee in Oakland, Ca. Aetna Life Insurance and Annuity Co. (10 years in management, 28 years Insurance and Financial Services).

Licenses, Professional Designations; LUTCF, currently enrolled in RICP with The American College.

Honors / Awards; Perennial MDRT, Leaders Conference with Aetna, MetLife, and Mass Mutual. NAIFA Board member Sacramento Chapter, African American Advisory council with both MetLife and MassMutual. Chair of African American Financial Advisors Group Northern California MassMutual Agency. Also, National Eagle Scouts Association, BSA. Ordained Elder in the AME Zion Church. (Received many awards and recognitions in ministry, both locally and nationally)

Social Media Links; Linked In.

Articles, Books Interviews; Panelist and Presenter at the CAAFP.

Family Background; Married for 37 years to Yasmin Williams, one daughter Ashley age 35 whom is a CBS Reporter.

Why did you choose this field?

Actually, the field chose me. I was in my 3rd year of college and a recruiter called to gauge my interest in the field of Insurance. I consented to an interview, took two aptitude battery tests, and based on the results was told I had a high probability of success in the field of Life Insurance sales. I was hired as a salaried Sales Management trainee in 1982. My job was to learn the business in the area of Life Insurance sales, recruiting and train new advisors. During this period, I recruited a number of Black Insurance agents, many of whom are still in business to this day. This was a successful venture for about 10 years. I discovered in this process that I had a skill set that warranted being a self-employed Financial Advisor. I left management in 1992 and never looked back. One area of focus as a manager and then as an advisor was to create marketing opportunities that gave me a steady stream of prospects. I thank God for the opportunity afforded me as a young Black man in Oakland Ca. The company was Aetna Life Insurance and Annuity Company, and they really allowed me to fly. It was during these years that taught me the value of truly helping people to protect what's important to them.

What experience caused you to consider leaving the industry?

Truth be told, I never considered leaving the field. When times were tough, I simply made more calls, booked more appointments and took some risks. I learned early in my career that this business is really recession proof. When there was 8 % unemployment, that meant there was 92% of Americans working. That means there was always somebody that could be a prospect/client. Even today, when there is a slow period, I would do my best to go see someone. Even if no sale occurred, the idea of sharing and offering advice gave me some confidence. So here I am, 38 years later, still loving what I do.

What's the "Standard" for our Industry?

I believe the Insurance Industry has established a remarkable level of trust in the eye of the public. They have the resources to replace incomes, rebuild burned down homes, replace incomes for someone disabled, etc... with that level of backing, the standard for Agents should be to position themselves as the professional that will help clients protect what's most important to them. And to accomplish this in the most ethical and cost-efficient manner. I believe clients expect the same thing. They want to work with someone who has their best interest at heart. I have learned in my years in the business that clients can tell if you really care or just want to make a sale. When our clients feel that high standards are prevalent, they have no problem sending you referrals from their own family and friends. I also believe that organizations like MDRT, NAIFA, GAMA and the American College really promote high standards for the industry. It is up to Financial Professionals to hold those standards up on a daily basis. As it applies to standards, there is a question that is raised by consumers concerning all of the labels that advisors use. I believe people are very confused by the number of designations in our industry. While working to become educated in your craft, and striving to get your CLU, ChFC, CFP, RICP, etc... The value of high standards is not just couched in designations. Integrity, honesty and genuine care for the needs of people should always come first. Now having said this, we should be careful not to belittle an agent that does not have labels after their name. This is where the confusion is manifested. Agent and client relationships are built on trust. When clients trust the financial professional and the company they represent, good things happen for both sides. To answer the second concern about the industry restricting the use of titles? I do think there should be some combination of labels. In other words, if you have CLU, you are no better or worse than an advisor with a CFP designation. The American College does a wonderful job in the areas of training and education for those who want to perfect their craft. Titles are here to stay, unless FINRA decides to place limits on them.

What % of your clients are black?

I would estimate approx. 40%. Some is by choice and some by default. I have done numerous workshops in many companies where there are black employees. I have noticed that many will gravitate to an advisor that's professional, well trained, somewhat successful, looks like them and understands the culture. Also, as a minister in the AME Zion Church, I have conducted many seminars and workshops in the area of financial literacy and management of resources. I never conducted these to get clients, however inevitably, many people have called on me over the years to help with their financial planning. I do however feel in this modern day in time, more African Americans in the workforce are willing to work with an advisor that represents their culture. This is also an opportunity for Financial Service Organizations to recognize a growing trend, and recruit to it. I have been blessed to find a couple of unique marketing niches. Years ago, I worked with an organization that focused on working with federal government employees. We learned how to set up a payroll deduction program through a national bank that allowed government employees to purchase Insurance and savings plans through their paycheck. We also took time to understand gaps in their coverages. I began by doing cold calls to HR managers at Social Security Admin, U. S. Postal Service and a number of VA Hospitals. We offered benefits education workshops at lunch time, and then offered one on one consultations. This was a very successful marketing program that was maximized for many years. I still think it can be worked by advisors even today. This was a unique market because many African Americans worked for Federal

Agencies. They were always happy to work with a black advisor, provided they were professional in their approach, speech and attire. By the way, I always wore a suit and tie. It presented a professional image, and most people, black and white appreciated this. Over the years I perfected this idea with other small businesses and corporations. If I had to do it all over again, I would work the same way, except I may do more of it. The skill set required to work in this space is really a full knowledge of how a target companies benefits actually work. This type of marketing also opens the door to working with persons approaching retirement. I still work this way; except I tend to target an older population that has a larger income and asset base to work with.

Early in my career, I did have a few situations where I had some difficulty getting clients from different races. I think this was really due to my own lack of faith in my own abilities. It was always "easy "to approach my own people. There was an assumption that white people with money would not trust working with a black financial professional. This was a fair assumption because the industry was very white male dominated. And in many respects, it is still that way today. However, the trends are shifting. People want to be listened to, and respected. These traits are color blind. Once I realized this, which took some time, and as my confidence increased, I realized I needed to be an advisor for everyone I had an opportunity to work with. There's always that one or two that just would not want to work with a black advisor. Oh well, their loss. There's an old saying, some will, some won't, so what.

If you were not able to acquire clients of other races, what impact would it have had on your overall wealth?

Wow, that's a good question. The short answer is that I would have established myself in the larger Estate planning arena, and Corporate Insurance opportunities. Also, my average case size would have been much higher, much earlier. Many advisors that are new in the business, tend to work with people on the lower end of the economic ladder. Many underserved families have a great desire to plan, but just can't afford it. When clients buy, and then cancel their policies, this has a very negative effect on the Advisors business. Early in my career, I learned some valuable lessons about persistency. I needed to make sure a new client could afford and sustain the products I was selling them. While in most cases, the client appeared to have the means and resources, often times the client just did not see the plan as a priority. This can be easily solved by proper training and doing what's right for the client. The beauty of Financial Planning in today's world is that it helps the client see very clearly where they are now, and points them to where they ultimately want to be, financially.

Are Black Financial Service Professionals hindered in their pursuit of building wealth? If so, what are the factors that impact it?

I don't believe we are hindered from a context of ability. I think many Black Financial professionals are challenged when working with management or sales trainers that don't understand our culture. If a Black sales manager that's successful in his field, is the trainer and manager of a new black Advisor, I think there is a higher probability of success. I am cautious with this question because I do believe that success comes from preparation, training and hard work. We must put the time in. At the same time, if there is a disconnect between manager and advisor with regard to "social comforts", it puts a strain on the relationship. I have seen many companies with thousands of Financial Professionals and maybe 2-3 % are Black. I have also noticed a very small percentage of the black advisors struggling to make minimum production, let alone company leaders conference and MDRT. This is an area of concern and opportunity for upper management in our industry. I also believe that we as Financial Professionals should make sure we buy what we sell. How much Life Insurance do we own? How solid is our retirement plan? Wealth for the Financial Professional often times comes with owning what we tell our clients to own. I think we can all do better in this area.

Is the generational wealth transfer of Black Financial Service Professionals in jeopardy due to an inability to acquire clients of other races?

I would say no. If anything, we need to have more young people join our industry. African Americans in this country have excelled far beyond the expectations of many. We are in every facet of corporate America. We represent the highest spending amongst most ethnic groups. We have the money, but many are poor stewards over what they have. I see some trends that support the idea of Black people becoming more educated about planning and investments. I think as Companies highlight the successes they have amongst the Advisors of color; people will gravitate to them.

The American College for Financial Services has a Scholarship targeted towards African-Americans to increase the numbers of us in the field. What other incentives do you think our industry can put in place to achieve this goal?

Wow, another big question. I think there are many incentives Individual companies can do, but as an industry, there should be a paradigm shift on what a financial professional look like. It's not just the White entrepreneur in a nice suit, it's also the face of a Black man or woman in a big office conducting business with clients. Perception is everything. If people have an image that's positive of Blacks-in business, they will have no problem working with us. If our image is always tainted in a negative context, well, you know the answer. Clearly more upper management, board room positions and even middle managers previously dominated by whites will give us an equal playing field.

Were you given an opportunity to intern with a more experienced advisor? If so, where and when?

Truth be told, I never was given this opportunity directly. I did however receive high quality training from the companies I represent. It was up to me to transform my training into prospecting. I am convinced that mentorship in today's business is vital. Even at the writing of this periodical, I am searching for a candidate to mentor and ultimately take over my practice. The average age for Financial Professionals is in the upper 50's to mid-60's. This creates a huge opportunity for young African Americans to enter our business. I will say this, they need to have a comfort in crossing multiple ethnic lines. Today's Financial Professional is not just for black people, we are for all people. With the advent of social media and electronic marketing schemes, often times the client is not sure what your race is. They can however tell if you know what you are talking about. They can also tell if you care about them and their situation.

What advice would you give an undergrad student who was considering financial services/planning as a career?

First of all, I would ask an undergrad why they want to be in this field. If it's purely financial, I would try and encourage them to rethink their motives. While this business has major financial rewards for those who succeed, it's not just about the money. I would help a new recruit understand it's really about helping people. The more people you help, the more you can make. In addition to this, I would share that the first few years are learning years. You must be willing to invest the first 2 to 3 years in development of your craft. In addition, you need to really like people. I have seen many in our industry love the chase or the opportunity, but they don't like people. People now days are much more educated about money and planning options, as they have access to numerous resources. If you can't differentiate yourself from others, why would someone want to work with you? How do you stand out in a crowd? What makes you better? These are questions that need to be understood and answered by a new advisor. After this level of deep conversation, then I would share with them, "This is the best business and Industry in The World". We get to set our own hours, work as much or as little as we want, and do great things to change the lives of millions. Truth be told, our industry is one of few where you can create a million-dollar estate with the stroke of a pen. As an addendum to this question for those who are new to the industry, if I could take a "mulligan" on my career, what would I do different. There's an old adage, if I knew then what I know now, oh what a feeling. I think if I could go back and redo some things, I think for starters I would actually have gotten some credentials early. I mean the one or two that people actually understood; ChFC® and CLU® were highly respected back then. As a young black new agent, the desire was really to learn and build a practice, which meant to make calls, set appointments see the people, and make sales. I think I would have used an experienced producer to help me with the more advanced markets. The Corporate and business market has always been where the big money is, I was not equipped nor comfortable in that arena. I am now, but it's taken a very long time to have conversations with people and tell them to write a check for $100,000. Honestly besides these two things, I would not make a change. Everything I have learned and put into practice can now be shared with new advisors coming into the industry. In addition, everything that worked in the 80's and 90's, still work today. People then were not as educated about financial matters, now days they are. But the gap is information overload. People have so much access to information, that it is confusing to the average consumer. That's where we come in to offer help, direction and advice.

In conclusion, I have been blessed to have had the opportunity to build a successful career in the Financial Services industry. I am truly thankful for all of the people that helped me along the way. They were colleagues, managers, clients and family. But mostly I thank God for his continuous blessings over my life. There were many times where I needed a lift to close the year out strong, and the Lord made a way out of no way. There were times I was over whelmed with my duties as a Pastor, a Presiding Elder and a husband and father. It was during those times that my faith gave me strength to persevere. I am convinced that our business is truly about teaching and helping people to navigate life in the realm of financial success. I was able to do this, as this business is really a ministry. When someone died and they wanted to make sure the policy they bought years ago was in force, the first one they call is their agent. When you get that call, you need to be ready to bring them joy and peace in their time of need. I have done this on hundreds of occasions. This is what really brings me joy, to be the one that can tell a widow or a family, "go ahead and make plans, the money is there". At the same time, I tell them my motto for life, "This is the day the Lord has made, go now and make the most of it".

Latoya Maddox

Professional Biography

- Educational background:

Undergraduate – Georgia State University Liberal Arts (Pre-law)/Minor in African American Studies

Executive MBA – Georgia State University – Robinson College of Business

- Years in the industry: 24 years (26 if I count my first job at Travelers)
- Licenses, professional certifications or designations
    - Certified Financial Planner designation
    - Property Casualty and Life and health Insurance License
    - Series 7

- Series 65

- Social Media links

Linked In: https://www.linkedin.com/in/latoyamaddox/

Facebook: https://www.facebook.com/infinityfinancialllc

Twitter: @mrscfp

Married to Donald Maddox and we have three children (Logan, Joshua, and Joseph)

Why did you choose this field?

I have always been keen on helping others, and while working to support myself through undergrad in insurance sales, I was drawn to the holistic idea of financial planning as it incorporated insurance, investments, strategic planning, and relationship building--I was hooked!

What experiencc caused you to consider leaving the field? What made you stay?

I never considered leaving the field. However, I did suffer from burnout and imposter syndrome. At the time, I felt that I was not growing as fast as I should. It was hard to connect with new clients because I started from scratch. I am originally from Chicago (Moved to Atlanta when I was 19 years old). As a result, I did not have a natural network. I tried to interview with a few firms and could not pass the litmus test of naming 20 of your closest friends. After bumping my head a few times in that direction, I knew the independent route was my best choice.

What would you consider the “standard” for our industry?

The standard for our industry is very hard to say. The beauty of financial services is that it spans a wide range of topics: risk management, taxes, estate, retirement, etc. Even these sections have multiple areas it can spin-off to that could serve a niche market. For me, I would say the standard is a deep set of values and ethics, continuous education (because things change daily in our business), a great attitude, and a servant leadership style.

What do you perceive the consumer sees as the “standard”?

A think the consumer is just not sure about one well-defined standard either. The CFP® has been branded as the standard when it comes to grading or ranking the professionals within the industry. However, an advisor may have experience in an area of finance that speaks to their individual needs. The consumer is looking for the best advisor to handle their unique situation. Do you think the average consumer is confused by all of the labels advisors use? Do you think the industry should restrict the use of “titles”? Yes, I think the consumer is confused and it is our job to explain our roles and relationship to the consumer. I like the CFP Board’s “Gold Standard” campaign. It sets it up that at minimum the consumer should work with a Certified Financial Planner and from this baseline, find a planner that specializes in their needs. Think of it like a general practitioner doctor vs a specialist. At minimum you want to see a doctor for general health and wellbeing. However, if you have a heart problem you will seek out a cardiologist (specialist)

Approximately what percentage of your clients are Black? Is this by choice or default?

I would say about 75% of my clientele are black as they are a part of my natural network of family and community connections. I generate the majority of my business through referral activity which creates a virtuous cycle within our small, tight-knit community. The other 25% of my clients are highly diverse and an outgrowth of strategic marketing and promotional activities to the other communities such as alumni, civic, and social organizations that I also belong to. Elaborate on your niche. What is it? Why this group? What skillsets are necessary to work with this group? I struggled in this area. My original plan was to work with families to increase their financial literacy, net worth, and help them prepare for retirement. I wanted to work with everyone. After working with a market strategist, she encouraged me to niche down. I was terrified at the thought but understood that I could not be all things to all people. I looked inside my firm and found the similarities of my clients and niched down from there. My clients are primary women between the age of 40 and 55. Executive or small business owners who are usually going through a transition when they seek me out for advice. Transitions are changing jobs, divorce, thinking about retiring, coming into an inheritance, or getting the kids out of the home and want to focus on themselves. An area I want to explore more is the medical industry. Specifically, nurses, pharmacists, and physical therapists. They have a great need and are often limited on the amount of time they can devote to their finances due to demands on their schedule.

The skillset needed to work with this group is a life planning approach and background in student loan debt repayment options. Really getting to what matters for the client. Money is just a tool to accomplish their many goals and milestones. Each client is different. My job is to find out their story and help them connect the dots on how to achieve what they need and steer clear of the financial landmines (job loss, unexpected death, medical scares, market shocks, inflation, etc.) along the way.

Would you take the same approach if you had to start over? I would have probably focused on a niche sooner. It is much easier to write blogs, social media posts, and put on seminars if you know exactly who you are speaking to.

What roadblocks have you had acquiring clients of other races?

People do business with whom they know, like, and trust. I do not actively seek out clients based on race but on common interests. I look for authentic connections with my clients outside of the services I offer. There is a mutual respect that develops as we work together to not only solve their financial challenges but also on other important issues.

If you were not able to acquire clients of other races, what impact do you think it would have on your overall wealth?

None, it is important for advisors to know there is not a scarcity of clients. We must create a profile of our ideal client and market to them.

My real answer is black advisors do not have to think we need to work with other races to make it. There is enough black wealth and through strategic relations you can naturally pick up clients with interest that align with yours.

Are Black Financial Services Professionals hindered in their pursuit of building wealth? If so, what are the factors that impact it?

I don't think so at all...I think we must get clear on who are the clients that are naturally drawn to us and market to them.

Is the generational wealth transfer of Black Financial Services Professionals in jeopardy due to an inability to acquire clients of other races?

Again, I don't think so. There are enough clients that we can market to that align with our values

The American College for Financial Services has a scholarship targeted towards African-Americans to increase the numbers of us in the field. What other incentives do you think our industry can put in place to achieve this goal?

Formal mentorship program at firms. Pairing a Senior African American advisor with an up-and-coming junior advisor. Ideally, the Senior planner can help start the young advisor out with smaller accounts so that the advisor can learn the art of managing client relations as they grow into larger engagements. This could be accomplished using a revenue sharing arrangement.

Were you given an opportunity to intern with a more experienced advisor? If, so, where and when?

I was not given the opportunity to intern. However, I met a Senior Advisor when I first started. He was an investment advisor and portfolio manager working with high-net-worth clients and I wanted to focus on financial planning. He helped me learn about investments by showing me how he used tactical analysis. This back in early 2000s when it was not widely discussed. He was generous with his time and other resources and became a mentor. He shared his office space and technology stack giving me access to tools and resources I never would have had at this stage in my career. It was a blessing, and truly a big deal! It gave me a level of credibility as I sought out new clients that made all the difference.

What advice would you give an undergrad student who was considering financial services/planning as a career?

The advice I give to all new advisor/planners:

Remember to be yourself – the industry is already challenging. So don't add the challenge of not being true to you.

Have multiple ways to generate income: sell insurance, prepare taxes to start (this is a good way to enter the financial lives of the right client), financial planning (of course), and don't be afraid to take a rollover IRA or small account that is not as large as you may like (these accounts grow overtime as the relationships grows).

Decide if you can work in the big firms or if you need to go hang your own shingle (It's all about the culture).

Again, do not think you need to fit in. It is ok to be different. It's an asset.

If you could take a "mulligan" on your career, what would you do differently?

I would have learned to collaborate earlier in my career. It would have been a much easier road had I found 2 -3 planners to partner with and build a firm. We each could have bought our strengths to the table. Instead, I became a master networker creating a strategic network of professionals to help service clients. It was more challenging but worked out in the end.

Ellis Liddell

Professional Biography

Ellis Liddell is the President and CEO of ELE Wealth Management, Inc. a client-based asset management company with its corporate office in Southfield, Michigan. With over 30 years of experience in the financial arena, Ellis is a wealth manager, insurance expert, and retirement planning specialist. He is author of the book, "Wealth Management: Merging Faith with Finance."

In 2007, Ellis Liddell became the first African American to be ranked the #1 financial advisor two years in a row at a nationally ranked investment firm.

He conducts financial seminars and workshops all across the country to businesses and churches alike, including Comerica Bank, Ford Motor Company, and TD Jakes' The Potter's House to name a few.

Ellis Liddell's brand of financial planning is uniquely rooted in sound financial and Biblical principles. He presents complex financial information in layman's terms, giving clients and seminar participants a wealth of knowledge, some homespun humor, and common sense.

✓ Educational background – Bachelor of Science, Mississippi College. Completed CFP program – Oakland University, Auburn Hills, MI

✓ Years in the industry – 31 Years

✓ Licenses, professional certifications or designations - Series 6, 7, 24, 28, 63, 65, Life & Health Insurance; Mortgage Loan Originator

✓ Honors/Awards –

- Proclamation Acknowledgement from U.S. Congress member Brenda Lawrence – 2018
- Proclamation Acknowledgement from City of Southfield Mayor Kenson J. Siver – 2018
- Top of the Table Qualifier- Million Dollar Round Table 2014 - Present
- Entrepreneur of the Year – Alabama A& M University – 2010

- Congressional Recognition from U.S. Senator Debbie Stabenow – 2010
- Letter of Acknowledgement from House of Representatives member, John Conyers Jr. - 2010
- Top producer Investment Advisor – Investors Capital Corporation 2006 and 2007
- #1 producer at National Life of Vermont (2002), #4 at National Life (2003), #2 at National Life (2004)
- Proclamation from the City of Atlanta and Rutherford County in Tennessee
- Received key to the city of Greenville, South Carolina

✓ Social Media links - www.linkedin.com/in/ellis-liddell-65ab2032

✓ Articles/Books/Interviews – Author – Wealth Management: Merging Faith with Finance. Contributing author to two other published works. Contributing Financial commentator to Detroit Smart Pages.

Why did you choose this field?

I would say that the field chose me. I have always had an interest in finance and at age 12 I started picking up financial books, magazines and reading items of that nature including my mom's tax return. At 12, I then started preparing her tax returns, and accurately I might add. Having grown up in Mississippi, it was so important to me that I broke the holds of poverty that held my family back for well over 100 years. Most of my family had never traveled 25 miles away from their birthplace; I dreamt of traveling the world. As of this writing, I am scheduled to travel to Antarctica which will represent seven continents I have visited throughout my journey.

What experience caused you to consider leaving the field? What made you stay?

At the start of my practice, the challenge with finding clients meant I did not have a niche. Once I developed my niche, clients started searching me out instead of the reverse. After 30 plus years of being in the industry, helping people to live a comfortable retirement, bury their loved ones, and send kids to college are some of my clients' successes and the greatest thank you I could ever receive.

Elaborate on your niche. What is it? Why this group? What skillsets are necessary to work with this group?

I consider myself as a retirement planning specialist which means I am interested and keep abreast with every single article, news report and conversation relating to retirement. My preferred age group is between age 55 – 65.

I call this the transition period. It is where I help individuals to pay down debt, enhance savings, and make tough decision about what retirement life looks like. Retirement, unfortunately, is one of those things that you only do once if done right. This requires conversations, often tough ones, to set and plan a retirement date. Retirement planning to me is like a huge jigsaw puzzle with all these small pieces needing to come together at a future point in time. There are going to be challenges along the way; however, seldom are they things that we planned for. As part of your planning, you must have a serious conversation with your clients regarding health planning. DNA in most cases serves as a great barometer of what future events we can anticipate from a health perspective. I take great pride in being able to answer questions with my clients regarding everything financial.

An insurance license, although not required, is very helpful in understanding the numerous types of insurance products needed to carry a person through life and into retirement. Series 65 – allows you to bill for services rendered. Series 6 or 7 – gives you a greater understanding on how securities actual work and allows you to cover the gamut of products available to fit your client's needs. There are also many other certifications that I feel will help you along the way based on personal goal and business practice.

If you are considering specializing in retirement planning as a specialty, I would recommend familiarizing yourself with the landscape. In every town/city there are employers who have specific plan documents for their employee benefit plans. My advice would be to get copies of all those plans to understand the specifics and nuances of what is required to retire those individuals. This puts you in the driver's seat and affords a great opportunity to create your niche.

What would you consider the "standard" for our industry?

Please keep in mind that everyone and every organization is trying to sell you something. The life insurance industry would like to have every agent have a CLU® (Chartered Life Underwriter) designation; the financial planning industry would like to have everyone have a CFP® (Certified Financial Planner) designation and the standard for the securities industry is a Series 7 license and it does not stop there. The million-dollar roundtable was established to represent the best of the best life insurance agents in the world and for them, the elusive top of the table became their covenant standard, not based on licensure but based on actual annual commission sales of $1M becoming their minimum standard. Each year thousands of representatives from around the world strive for and exceed the standard and each year they renew their membership with the organization. The organization holds conferences, webinars, trainings all of which are designed to help individuals achieve maximum success which is the desire of all organizations. Whichever standard you chose will be the one that you compare yourself to as you assist your clients in achieving their goals. When it's all said and done, we are here to serve others and give back to our communities.

What do you perceive the consumer sees as the "standard"?

I think the average consumer is still accustomed to the life insurance agent who comes to their house and sits at the kitchen table and makes a recommendation about what product best fits their needs. I still encounter clients who have found their way to my office or contacted me but have no idea how I can best serve them. I think that we have a great opportunity as African American advisors to lead the charge of educating our family and friends about the benefits that we can bring to them in achieving their goals and visions.

Do you think the average consumer is confused by all of the label's advisors use? Do you think the industry should restrict the use of "titles"?

I think the labels are designed to let consumers know your chosen area of specialty. For example, I have seen individuals use the title retirement consultant or college planning professional. No matter what the chosen title, it is designed to be an indication of your area of specificity. I have simply chosen the title of president, which has allowed me the luxury as well as the courtesy of serving thousands of clients with whom I am able to match a specific situation with the appropriate product or service.

I believe the industry has evolved because of their openness, allowing individuality in a space that has been quite rigid for years. When I entered the industry some 40 plus years ago, there were mainly only two titles - life insurance agent or stockbroker. There are more opportunities for the representative no matter what they call themselves to earn an exceptional income that far exceeds most industries today. Some 40 years ago, I never thought it was possible for a representative whether they were a life insurance agent or stockbroker to earn a 7 or 8 figure income. With the population growth as well as greater financial awareness, over the next 10-20 years 7 or 8 figure incomes will be the expectation not a dream. What does Amazon make? Money! There is no product associated with Amazon. Because of that openness and not being defined by titles, it allowed them to become the world's biggest store.

Approximately what percentage of your clients are Black? Is this by choice or default?

99% of my clients are black and it is by choice. I spent 10 years working for other financial institutions and did not have a single black client which led me to start my firm and commit myself to serving the African American community. Quite often, the African American market is overlooked as there is a perception that we do not have money to invest which I know not to be true. What is lacking and needed; however, is financial literacy. In my practice, I have leveled the playing field by eliminating account minimums and offering thousands of free consultations. Over the years, I have advised numerous couples that at the time could only afford life insurance but as they have advanced in their careers, they came back to invest with me because I did not put a price tag on my service.

Would you take the same approach if you had to start over?

Absolutely. When I started, talk radio was just gaining popularity. There were not many financial experts on talk radio. Therefore, I decided that I would become one of them. I have made numerous appearances on many media platforms based on my decision that I would be the go-to person in my community. My desire was to help as many people as possible by educating our community on the various financial solutions available and to even shed light on understanding the term wealth management. As I wrestled with an appropriate name for my business over 20 years ago, the big decision back then was whether to become ELE Asset Management or ELE Wealth Management. I settled for ELE Wealth Management before anyone in the country used "Wealth Management" to describe their business. My website was the first to define what wealth management was to me. One statement listed on my website has been duplicated around the world and that is "wealth management is a holistic approach to one's life".

What roadblocks have you had acquiring clients of other races?

I made a commitment to serve the African American community; therefore, all my marketing and focus have been centered around that segment of the population. Even though, I have stayed within my niche market; other cultures have sought me out based on hearing me on the mediums and markets in which I chose to advertise and market my business; particularly talk radio. Although I am a frequent guest on the local ABC TV affiliate, I have not chosen to ask for clients from that association.

If you were not able to acquire clients of other races, what impact do you think it would have on your overall wealth?

By dealing exclusively with the African American community, I have escaped the woes that many advisors suffer due to unconscious bias. When one of my African American clients refers one of their non-African American friends to us, we do not have to concern ourselves about any kind of bias because their African American friend has prepared them for the African American experience, and they have chosen to do it consciously. I believe my wealth is much better because this is the niche I have chosen, and my clients have rewarded me for that conscious choice.

Are Black Financial Services Professionals hindered in their pursuit of building wealth? If so, what are the factors that impact it?

Absolutely not. When I chose to become a retirement planning specialist some 20 years ago and after thousands of clients later, I can look back and truly say that the only limitations to becoming a top producer at any firm, be it your own or someone else's, is the limitation you place on yourself. I think that most advisors approach the industry as if they are playing checkers when their approach should be as playing chess. Chess requires strategizing and anticipating your counter moves as well as those of your opponent. After being #1 at Investors Capital Corporation two consecutive years and #1 at National Life of Vermont and being in the top 5 of any organization I have been affiliated while servicing African American clients, I cannot imagine my wealth and my legacy being any greater than serving any other community than my own. Each day when I awake knowing that I have touched tens of thousands of African Americans who will never look at wealth the same way again, it is a reflection of our motto which has drawn more new clients to us than any other marketing campaign by simply using the words and living to what they say..." Wealth is our legacy, pass it on!"

Is the generational wealth transfer of Black Financial Services Professionals in jeopardy due to an inability to acquire clients of other races?

Based on 2019 statistics, the African American population in America is over 46.8 million. Because of that population growth, which should continue to grow, African American advisors who chose to serve their own communities, will enjoy a greater sense of inclusion and success by serving people who both appreciate their professionalism and their level of education as it relates to financial services.

The American College for Financial Services has a scholarship targeted towards African-Americans to increase the number of us in the field. What other incentives do you think our industry can put in place to achieve this goal?

I think each one, teach one; each one, reach one, should be a part of our calling as African American advisors. This opens an avenue where we can teach the community the importance of financial literacy then they can encourage their children and their children's children to participate in this process. The same emphasis and encouragement should be placed on our profession as is given to other professionals such as doctors, lawyers, and engineers. After all, they also seek out the advice of financial advisors. At ELE, we have done just that. For the past 20 years, each summer we have provided paid internships to young people 15 years or older allowing them to shadow me along with my entire staff to get a better understanding of what it takes to run all aspects of a financial firm. Many of these interns had no idea about the rewards offered in the financial services industry; not to mention the potential of earning a higher-than-average income.

Were you given an opportunity to intern with a more experienced advisor? If, so, where and when?

Yes. It was an 18-month paid internship with a million-dollar producer in Dallas, TX, in July 1998. In the hiring process, he asked me one question that stopped me in my tracks. He asked, “Do you know how to market?” I tried to pivot and said I am a great salesperson. His response was, “anyone can sell if they have a warm body in front of them, but how do you get a warm body in front of you?” This is where most people fail because they do not know how to get clients. During the 18 months, I watched him through seminar marketing, writing newspaper articles, and appearing on local TV. But more importantly, I watched him have a confident attitude that without a doubt, he was the best financial advisor a client can have. I watched him do the work and enjoy the rewards of serving his clients and community. He was the kind of guy that wanted you to know that he was present, and he made sure that everybody he touched knew he was special. And even though personality plays a huge role in selling yourself, whether on a phone conference, zoom call, or in-person, I made the decision that I too would do the work and enjoy every reward that I am afforded.

What advice would you give an undergrad student who was considering financial services/planning as a career?

I would encourage them to work for an experienced advisor with 10-20 years in the industry even if you have to shadow that person because you don’t know what you don’t know. By working with an advisor, you get to practice (make your mistakes) while being in a training mode and being supervised because when you strike out on your own, mistakes can be quite costly.

If you could take a "mulligan" on your career, what would you do differently?

If I were allowed a mulligan, I would still utilize the procedures I have put in place, but I would be more confident in knowing I would achieve my dream goals. Because I believe that God is in control, every mistake, accomplishment, let down, unanswered prayer got me to this place in my career. I thank God for unanswered prayers as it related to a job I applied for. It is my fundamental belief that if I had a chance to do it all over again, I would bring the knowledge that everyone in your practice does not have to be a salesperson. To be a successful firm, you need an administrative staff, compliance officer and other essential personnel to create a well-oiled machine but not necessarily more salespeople.

Dr. Copeland, I would like to thank you for the opportunity and the consideration given to me to be included in this great work. Nothing like this existed in 1980 when I decided to enter this business. Words of wisdom that could have served as a guiding light for others to follow will go a long way to help our next generation bridge the gaps that are absolutely necessary for our community's success. Though every advisor brings a unique set of eyes from their journey, I am proud to say that my journey has been one of shared experiences and learning from others the power of knowing that if I ask for help, someone will gladly come forward. Thank you!

Intentionally Left Blank

Rene' Nourse

Professional Biography

Educational background – Bachelor's Degree from Oberlin College: the first college in the US that accepted Women and Blacks beginning in 1835.

Years in the industry – 35

Licenses, professional certifications or designations –

Founder/CEO – Urban Wealth Management Group, LLC and UWM Insurance Services, CFP®, Series 7 License and Insurance Professional

Honors/Awards – Charles Schwab National Ad Campaign, Marquis Who's Who, Los Angeles Times Banking & Finance Visionaries Group, Investment News Women to Watch, Five Star Professional Wealth Manager, Former President of Assn. of African American Financial Advisors, Guest commentator for CNBC Closing Bell Report 2013- 2019

Social Media links –
https://www.linkedin.com/in/renenourse/;
https://www.facebook.com/urbanwealthmanagement
https://www.instagram.com/urbanwealthmgt/
https://www.urbanwm.com/about-us/our-team/rene-nourse-cfp

Why did you choose this field?

I choose this field based on my personal experience as a child and young adult due to low-income levels and inability to adequately save and grow assets. My mother was truly inspirational- was divorced with 3 kids- and returned to a university to receive her Masters. However, due to of course, the lower income levels that women and people of color received AND that our father was not consistent in providing child support, she struggled with having enough money to pay for our family-related expenses. As a matter of fact, when I began working in my early teen years, periodically she would ask if she could borrow money from me to pay bills – and of course, always repaid me. As a result, I became focused on finding ways to build out a strong financial future for not just myself, but for my family and the next generation. Additionally, I saw that this was a big issue with many other families of color – and women.

What experience caused you to consider leaving the field? What made you stay?

In the early stages of my financial career, there were situations where people didn't want to work with me due to my skin color. Back in the day when I started in the industry, advisors were called stockbrokers and we generated our business via cold calling. So, when I spoke with folks, they knew that I was a woman – however, when they came into the office, they saw that I was black – they thought I was an assistant, and not the "stockbroker" they spoke with. In a few situations, they declined to work with me. Thankfully, my office managers were very supportive and told those individuals that if they didn't work with me, they couldn't work with anyone else in the office. So, while this was one circumstance for considering leaving the industry, there was another. It was difficult making enough money to support my lifestyle too, especially since I was divorced and a single mom. While there were times when I felt that I needed to leave the industry, the thought of having to learn other skillsets and tasks within other industries, was not compelling. So, I stayed and thankfully, it was the best decision.

What would you consider the "standard" for our industry?

The "standard" for the industry is one that needs to change. Instead of the financial industry focusing on working with high-net worth clients – we need to focus on the means of helping others who aren't "HNW", which understandably is predominantly people of color. The focus should be to assist in helping them to make better financial decisions, provide oversight for way to build out their wealth and providing legacy planning initiatives. ¬

What do you perceive the consumer sees as the "standard"?

The customer does see the above issue as standard and it is scary to many of them since they feel that many "advisors" won't work with them unless they have a significant amount of assets. What is more important and needs to change is the need to share that financial planning is different than financial/asset management services. That's what will make the difference for enhancing this industry to attract and maintain the relationship of the majority of this country's residents/customers/consumers.

Initially when I was thinking of "standard", I was thinking of CFP Designation, MDRT recognition, publications, etc. since there are so many different types of advisors. Please respond from the point of view of the professional & the client.

From the professional standpoint, having access to a handful vs hundreds of different designations is key. Many firms provide their own internal professional designation titles, which is often times not an industry based standard designation. I think it's important that the financial industry needs to provide sufficient oversight and directives about achieving certain training and designations. While from the investment professional standpoint, one must have specific licenses and designations, many consumers don't realize that. For clients, it's important for them to do background checks on their advisors - initially and periodically by going to Broker Check and/or SEC sites. Additionally, tracking your advisor/planner on social media sites, their website and also if they are on any podcast, webinar or have published any articles. It gives consumers/clients a great opportunity to know who their advisor really is.

Approximately what percentage of your clients are Black? Is this by choice or default?

Approximately 60%. Our clients are diversified – which means including all races. We are blessed in that respect.

What roadblocks have you had acquiring clients of other races?

None- my top ten clients are people of color: AA, Latin-X and Asian.

If you were not able to acquire clients of other races, what impact do you think it would have on your overall wealth?

N/A

Are Black Financial Services Professionals hindered in their pursuit of building wealth? If so, what are the factors that impact it?

Depending on the firm they work for, there could be a negative impact since these firms tend to make it a priority to focus on high net-worth clients. The majority of the clients we tend to serve are people of color -in particular, Blacks, who as we know are not paid as much as others who have the same background, education, experience as their white counterparts. As a result, many of these clients also have a high level of debt that we need to assist in clearing out: typically, student loan debt. As a result, unless the firm the professionals work for, are open to supporting this endeavor, it can be a challenge. Being an independent advisor, however, can assist in meeting Black Financial Services Professionals with their directives and desire to work with any one they wish to support.

Is the generational wealth transfer of Black Financial Services Professionals in jeopardy due to an inability to acquire clients of other races?

Personally, I don't think so. Due to the horrific cycle of 2020, many people – including whites – are interested in working with people of color professionals. At our firm, we have been contacted by individuals of various races – although primarily Black and Latin-X, who wish to work with our firm. Although last year was awful, there have been several positive changes that have occurred that will make a difference in this industry.

The American College for Financial Services has a scholarship targeted towards African-Americans to increase the numbers of us in the field. What other incentives do you think our industry can put in place to achieve this goal?

Ideally, our country needs to incorporate financial training in schools- beginning in elementary school. Kids already know how and what to spend money on but are not knowledgeable about the steps to create financial strength in their lives over the long term. The earlier one starts, the better off they will be. The financial industry can provide training for teachers/educators about areas and topics to cover with their students and create a series of classes so that these educators do not have to create it on their own. Additionally, I think it is extremely important for us as Black Financial Professionals to be actively engaged in these educational platforms, participate in the school's career services day- so that students can learn to "be what they can see". Often times, students elementary up through college, have no or little knowledge about this industry.

Were you given an opportunity to intern with a more experienced advisor? If, so, where and when?

No- but I have interned others.

What advice would you give an undergrad student who was considering financial services/planning as a career?

To be an intern and if possible, to focus on being interned with a person of color professional.

Elaborate on your niche. What is it? Why this group? What skillsets are necessary to work with this group?

Our firm focuses on women. Historically, women have been overlooked and underserved- on both the client and the professional advisor side. While often times, people think that working with women is a niche, that's not true since women are a network. From the standpoint of what "niches" our firm focuses on, it is professionals (who work for publicly traded companies, since it is important to understand how they can build out their wealth by understanding their benefits), educators and widows.

Do you think the average consumer is confused by all of the label's advisors use? Do you think the industry should restrict the use of "titles"?

Yes, I do think that consumers have been very confused by titles since there hasn't been a formalized recognition of who or what these professionals do. For example, I often have to explain the difference between what a financial advisor is vs. a financial planner since so many consumers believe they are the same professional that provides the same services. Financial Advisors tend to focus primarily on investments whereas financial planners provide services to help clients strengthen their financial life and they can also provide investment management services as well- which is what our firm provides.

Would you take the same approach if you had to start over?

The only difference I would have taken would have been to inaugurate my firm earlier in my professional career. While we will be celebrating 10 years in 2022, I would have loved for it to have been 20 years- which would have given me more time to build out a broad-based firm with many women - of different ethnicities, ages and lifestyles.

If you could take a "mulligan" on your career, what would you do differently?

Nothing- I began my financial career in the insurance industry, which provided substantial understanding on the foundational elements that many black people feel comfortable about getting, then moved into the investment industry- good starting point.

Gary Clements

Professional Biography

Gary O. Clement, CFP®, CRPS®, CRPC®, AFC®,MPAS®, is President of Clement Asset Management, LLC, a financial planning and investment management firm, a lead instructor in the Kaplan Schweser Certified Financial Planning Program, an adjunct professor at the College for Financial Planning, and an assistant professor at the University of Alabama. Gary is a Summa Cum Laude graduate of Cheyney University of Pennsylvania, a graduate of the Oglethorpe University Financial Planner Program, and holds a MSFS degree from the College for Financial Planning. Gary is currently pursuing a Ph.D. in financial planning at the University of Georgia.

Gary considers himself both a lifelong student and teacher of personal finance. He enjoys educating groups, large and small, about money, personal finance, and the myriad financial products, vehicles, and strategies available to them.

Over the past 20+ years, Gary has worked with discount brokers, independent broker-dealers, and wire houses. Today, Gary leads an independent registered investment advisory firm that focuses on comprehensive financial planning and investment management. He's held FINRA Series 7, 63, 65, 3, 31, and 24 licenses and has been a CERTIFIED FINANCIAL PLANNER since 2006. He's also taught Fundamentals of Financial Planning, Investment Management, Retirement Planning and Estate Planning courses for the Certified Financial Planning programs at Oglethorpe University, the Terry College of Business at the University of Georgia, and Kaplan Schweser. He has also taught in degree granting programs at the College for Financial Planning, Clark Atlanta University, the University of Georgia, and the University of Alabama.

LinkedIn: https://www.linkedin.com/in/garyoclement/

Why did you choose this field?

It's hard to say whether I chose financial services or financial services chose me. I always enjoyed learning about money and investing. Then, when I studied the topic personally, I got excited about the many different strategies that could be used to improve one's life. When I learned, further, that through a financial services career someone could do well for themselves while they were also doing good things for other people, I became convinced that a career in financial services was for me.

What experience caused you to consider leaving the field? What made you stay?

First of all, getting into the business was a challenge. After deciding that financial services were for me, I interviewed with several of the big wire house firms with no success. Shortly after that, I learned that a growing online discount broker, with a big footprint in my city, was hiring. From what I could tell, they were hiring anybody with a pulse. So, I threw my hat in the ring to see if I could get a start there and learn about the business from the inside. My plan was to work, learn, get fully licensed and move on - which is exactly what I did. I went from discount brokerage world to full service, when I finally got hired at a big wire house firm. While being with the wire house was a great experience, it was very difficult to build my assets under management. I did a lot of cold-calling and running around town meeting with potential clients. Still, it was very hard to build my book of business. I didn't feel like I got much support in trying to build business, either. This was circa 2001 through 200, so 911 played a role, as well. Of course, being with a wire house means that there was a lot of pressure to build your book of business. Unfortunately, I got laid off and it caused me to wonder if financial services were the business for me. I took some time to really think about that and I came to the conclusion that I really enjoyed the business. I just needed to figure out how to navigate this business in a way that I could not only succeed personally but also do what I thought was best to help other people.

What would you consider the "standard" for our industry?

In my mind, the Certified Financial Planner designation is the standard in the business. We all come from different silos in this business. If someone comes up in the investment world, they tend to look for investment-based solutions. If someone comes up in the insurance world, they tend to look for insurance solutions. If someone comes up in the tax accounting world, they tend to look for tax solutions. In other words, we all start out with myopia. It's as if we are carpenters with our only tool being a hammer. If that is the case, then every problem looks like a nail.

Anyone who has gone through the education, experience and testing process set forth by the CFP Board, they have achieved a feat that has also provided them a wide scope of knowledge that they can use to help people in real comprehensive ways. The bottom line is that there are a lot of ways to help clients meet their goals. And, you need to have exposure to a lot of information to determine, among the many alternatives, what may be the most efficient and effective ways to help clients meet their goals. For that reason, I do wholeheartedly believe that the CFP designation stands alone.

I think, though, that there is going to be a growing standard in the business - facility with behavioral finance. I've always told clients that personal finance is more "personal" than "finance" -- meaning it's more about their behavior than the numbers. And, I really believe that is 100% true. Certainly, financial planners can be better positioned to be of far greater value to clients by understanding the often-predictable ways clients make suboptimal financial decisions. And, by integrating behavioral finance into a financial planning practice, planners will be able to better explain, anticipate, and ameliorate client behavior. In a changing financial services landscape that features robo-advisors, internet technology, and zero commissions, dealing with the uniquely human aspects of financial planning, in my humble opinion, planners who have a good understanding behavioral finance are clearly the future of financial planning. There are uniquely human factors like emotions and empathy that become particularly important, and that only human beings can respond to, that will ensure that the CFP professional continues to be relevant to the population.

Let me make another point about that. The CFP Board puts forth a seven-step financial planning process. One, understanding the client's personal and financial circumstances; two, identifying and selecting client goals (guided by the client, of course); three, analyzing the client's current course of action and potential alternative courses of action; four, developing financial planning recommendations; five, presenting financial planning recommendations; six, implementing the recommendations; and, finally, monitoring the client's plan and progress towards their goals. I contend, though, that the last step could just as easily in "motivate". Because, if we cannot motivate clients to do what they need to do to achieve their goals, then all the rest of what we may do is worthless.

What do you perceive the consumer sees as the "standard"?

Of course, the CFP Board has raised awareness of the CFP designation and people are now beginning to ask whether advisors have the designation. But, by and large, most consumers are confused about the many distinctions between how advisors are licensed, registered, and how they may do business. Consumers, instead, tend to lump all advisors together. So, I think, even though what the CFP Board has done is laudable, most consumers still do not have a standard that they look for.

Approximately what percentage of your clients are Black? Is this by choice or default?

100% of my clients are African American. And, I hesitate to say that this by choice or default. Honestly, it's probably a little bit of both. We are taught, in this business, to start with your warm market. After that, you may then seek to cast a wider net. Also, part of the reason I got into this business was because I saw a need that was not being addressed. Financial advisors are greatly needed in the African American community. So, while I have not actively tried to attract much business outside of the African American community, I have had very few people from other communities seek me out. So, it's a little of both.

What roadblocks have you had acquiring clients of other races?

I'm sure there are plenty of roadblocks. I have, personally, purposefully avoided focusing on that, though. From a broader perspective, I can say that African American advisors are not held up in the media as financial experts. So, certainly, that impacts the perception of African American advisors. It influences people from other cultures when they are approached by African American advisors. But it also influences African American prospects, too. So, as a manner of speaking, African American advisors are placed in the position of constantly convincing people that their ice is as cold as the other guy's ice. That is a potential barrier to attracting a diverse clientele and it's an impediment to building business with African American client, too.

If you were not able to acquire clients of other races, what impact do you think it would have on your overall wealth?

Absolutely. Because we may be constricted by outside factors, just staying in business is the first challenge. If, as advisors, we cannot make money, we cannot stay in business. If we cannot make money, we are unable to help ourselves, let alone help anyone else. This is the reason that many advisors cycle through the business. This is particularly an issue for African American advisors.

We know the numbers. In aggregate, African Americans have a fraction of the wealth that White Americans have. So, we fish in a smaller pond. Figuring out how to deal with that is challenging.

Are Black Financial Services Professionals hindered in their pursuit of building wealth? If so, what are the factors that impact it?

Surely, African American financial services professionals are hindered in their pursuit of building businesses and building wealth. By and large, we enter this business with few advantages. We may not have family wealth to begin with. We may not have access to a wealthy network. This gets back to the realities of aggregate wealth in our community. This means that, though many advisors of all types cycle through the business, this is a particular challenge for African American advisors.

If advisors are unable to have long standing in the business in order to develop knowledge and experience, it impacts them greatly, and it, in turn, impacts their potential clientele. Another thing the impacts African American advisors negatively is the lack of support and mentoring that will allow them to enhance their ability to help clients and help them succeed in the business.

Is the generational wealth transfer of Black Financial Services Professionals in jeopardy due to an inability to acquire clients of other races?

I don't think so. I think that, if someone is determined enough to hang in and overcome tough times, they can build a successful business and do well for themselves and help plenty of clients. As we succeed at advising clients and helping them build wealth, we have an opportunity to help those that come after use - clients and advisors, alike.

As we advise clients, I think that our job is to educate clients, as well. What we should be doing is so far beyond financial products and strategies. Getting back to behavioral finance, can we deal with their observed and demonstrated behavior that maybe preventing them from reaching their wealth building potential. Another aspect of educating clients is helping them understand what is at stake for them, their children, grandchildren, and broader circles of influence. We should help people understand what they can do to not only help themselves and make their lives easier. More importantly, we should help people understand that they have the power to make the lives of those that come after them easier, as well. Take housing, for example. Many other communities help younger generations with down payment assistance on a first home. After a few years, and after building significant equity by paying off a portion of the mortgage and appreciation, they may sell the home and have their capital gains shielded as they buy a bigger and better home. Do this a few times, and you can see how real estate is a huge wealth accelerator that the African American community doesn't fully participate in. Now if we add missing out on endowments that come from life insurance, or bequests of significant real property or assets, we can see how each African American generation starts over from scratch. American Americans rarely inherit significant wealth. This impacts them and advisors, too.

The American College for Financial Services has a scholarship targeted towards African-Americans to increase the numbers of us in the field. What other incentives do you think our industry can put in place to achieve this goal?

Scholarships are important. But a real game changer is mentoring. The question is, how do we provide enough mentoring for young people who want to enter this business? How do we mentor people before they get their first job in the industry? How do we support them as they grow in the business? How do we advise them on career moves? How do we ensure that they will be in nurturing situations? This can happen at wire houses and at RIA firms, regardless of who is doing the mentoring.

Were you given an opportunity to intern with a more experienced advisor? If, so, where and when?

I have to laugh at this one! I did not have access to an experienced advisor willing to mentor me as I came along in the business. It has been all OJT (On the Job Training). It was a real missing, but it caused me to do all that I could to continually learn. There are plenty of resources for anyone willing to seek them out. In that sense, I have had a lot of unsuspecting mentors through the books, articles and interviews I read and seen. Starting with people like Nick Murray and Michael Kitces, I made it a point to learn as much as I could from readily available sources. I also had an interesting job on my path. I worked as an internal auditor for a large independent broker dealer network. I was tasked with auditing small independent advisors. For two years, before I started my audit, I sat down with each advisor and asked them how they got into the business, how they built their book of business, what best practices worked for them, and what, if anything, they would do differently if they if they were starting out anew? I found all of those I spoke with forthcoming about their experience, because no one ever asked them. That was a hugely wonderful experience that helped me tremendously. So, regardless of whether a young advisor has someone step forward to help them, they can find ways to learn formally and informally.

What advice would you give an undergrad student who was considering financial services/planning as a career?

Get in the game! It doesn't matter what your first job is, because that first job may not be their final job. Even though undergrad students may have gained a good degree of technical knowledge, they do not know the business. And, while their formal college education is coming to a close, informal life and career education are just beginning. In colloquial terms, "they don't know what they don't know." In light of that, a first job is just that - a first job. It will provide a new opportunity to learn. It will provide context for their career. And, it will provide a platform to compare varying present and future opportunities, with their current employer or with outside firms. In short, a first job shouldn't matter as much as the chance to get your feet wet in the industry and learn as much as possible. I would also say this, "Congratulations, you're a freshman, again!"

Elaborate on your niche. What is it? Why this group? What skillsets are necessary to work with this group?

I primarily work with African American women, ages 35 - 65+. I do that purposefully, because I have a great deal of faith in African American women, due to how they show up in the world for themselves, their families, and their broader communities. I also have a great deal of faith that whatever African American learn or gain through working with financial planners is more apt to be passed on. There is another reason, though, African American women are an ascending demographic. There are more than well represented in the ranks of new executives in corporate American and they are forging new paths as successful entrepreneurs. That has come with an impressive increase in income. Unfortunately, that increased income doesn't always translate into wealth. So, there is a lot of good work that can be done with African American women.

The skill set necessary to work with African American women is the same skill set it takes to effectively work with anyone. Active listening skills, counseling skills, behavioral finance knowledge, all are vital in working with African American women.

Do you think the average consumer is confused by all of the label's advisors use? Do you think the industry should restrict the use of "titles"?

Yes. But, let's distinguish between "titles" and "designations." I say that because most professional advisors are confused by this too. First, when discussing "titles,"

We have to acknowledge that they are virtually meaningless. Whether someone is a vice president, account executive, etc., it doesn't mean anything. If we constrain ourselves to the investment world, there are only two ways one can operate -- as a registered representative or a registered investment advisor. And, there are differences between how they operate.

As far as financial services designations, average consumers are very confused. But I think that the CFP Board, again, has done a wonderful job of highlighting the CFP designation and what value its holders can provide for consumers. Other designations are far less recognized. But I think that they can be very important, as well. Anyone who endeavors to obtain an advanced designation is making the all-important commitment to build their knowledge and skills. That is never a bad thing. Another thing that is important about designations is that they can be a form of advertising. Even though the average consumer may not know what a particular designation entails, it signals that the advisor is serious about continuing their education so that they can be well positioned to help their clients.

Would you take the same approach if you had to start over?

It is hard for me to envision what I would do differently - probably because I've been so engrossed in my ongoing experience. But, if I had to start, I'd probably do what I encourage my students to do: learn as much as possible, as soon as possible. This is a knowledge business. As they grow in the business, they will find what works for them and what doesn't. I think my former self would benefit from that advice, too.

If you could take a "mulligan" on your career, what would you do differently?

N/A

Intentionally Left Blank

Leida Speller

Professional Biography

✓ **Educational background**

Bachelor of Business Administration in International Business – American Intercontinental University

✓ **Years in the industry**

25

✓ **Licenses, professional certifications or designations** ✓

Series 6, 7, 63 and 24

CFP®, ChFC®, RICP®

✓ **Social Media links**
https://www.linkedin.com › leida-speller-cfp®

Why did you choose this field?

I chose this field out of deep curiosity and a desire to learn something I knew absolutely nothing about. I was a 22-year-old looking for a job and stumbled upon an employment ad in the local newspaper for a mutual fund establishing a call center in my city. The company was looking for shareholder services representatives. I didn't even know what a mutual fund was, and it really piqued my interest. I was a part of the inaugural group of new employees opening the site. I was fortunate to be selected as a trades representative in an environment with a strong employee development culture, and to have the opportunity to cultivate relationships with the country's top investment firms.

What experience caused you to consider leaving the field? What made you stay?

My first 20 years in this industry were spent in a wide variety of industry functions, including Operations, Trading, and Client Relationship and Practice Management. I even spent several years running financial capability programs for a national nonprofit organization. I must say that, by far, being out front as an entrepreneur building my own practice has been the most difficult. It has challenged me in many ways. I have had to expand my comfort zone, develop new skill sets and contend with financial insecurity I had not seen since I was that 22-year-old looking for a job. The insecurity of not having a consistent, every-two-weeks' paycheck was, at times, a lot for me to bear – even after having planned for it financially. I found watching my reserves dwindle with uncertainty as to when they would be replenished extremely stressful.

I have stayed the course because I am passionate about the difference I make in my community. I see, every single day, how much I need my community and my community needs me. Representation and relatability are critical. Advocacy on behalf of the underserved is as necessary today as it was 50 years ago. I feel purposed in the work of increasing the financial capability and long-term wellbeing of African Americans. I believe that as a skilled, highly qualified advisor, I have so much to offer – in many ways and arenas.

What would you consider the "standard" for our industry?

I consider the "standard" for our industry, in terms of practicing professionals, to be an individual who does this work with the highest of integrity, puts the best interest of the client first, and commits to ongoing education and professional development. The minimum bar I set for myself was to combine my years of experience in the industry with the accomplishment of earning the CFP® designation.

What do you perceive the consumer sees as the "standard"?

I perceive the consumer's standard is someone they perceive as being knowledgeable and trustworthy.

Approximately what percentage of your clients are Black? Is this by choice or default?

I would say at least 95% of my clients are Black. Though I am intentional about offering education and literacy opportunities in the Black community, I would consider the current configuration of my book as being by default, rather than choice. I am honored to serve any race, creed or culture who finds value in the services I provide.

What roadblocks have you had acquiring clients of other races?

The most significant roadblocks have been the fact that my natural market is predominantly Black, and having limited access to marketing resources and expertise I believe would make an impact on my ability to reach a broader prospecting base.

If you were not able to acquire clients of other races, what impact do you think it would have on your overall wealth?

As a professional for whom investment advisory fees serve as the foundation of recurring revenue, I do believe the inability to acquire clients of other races, over time, would negatively impact my overall wealth. The country's wide racial wealth gap contributes to this. While this is true, I make a good living serving the population I serve. More important, I feel very purposed and called in my work.

Are Black Financial Services Professionals hindered in their pursuit of building wealth? If so, what are the factors that impact it?

I believe this to be true, primarily because generating sufficient revenue requires well-established markets that offer prospects financially capable of consuming the services we provide. This often requires the ability to build relationships and create opportunities within communities that may prefer to work with professionals who look like them.

Is the generational wealth transfer of Black Financial Services Professionals in jeopardy due to an inability to acquire clients of other races?

While I don't know that I would use the phrase "in jeopardy", I do believe that for the average Black Financial Services Professional, wealth accumulation and the ability to transfer wealth to the next and future generations becomes more difficult.

The American College for Financial Services has a scholarship targeted towards African-Americans to increase the numbers of us in the field. What other incentives do you think our industry can put in place to achieve this goal?

I think the scholarship programs are admirable. I do hope students are taking advantage of them. A strong consumer base in our natural markets is critical to the success of African American Financial Services Professionals. It is also scarcer than in other populations. I believe that showing yourself as a strong advocate of equity and equality in the areas of income and professional opportunities on behalf of the African American community can make a difference. Again, our opportunities for success are increased when we have more consumers in the marketplace who are financially capable and likely to do business with us.

Were you given an opportunity to intern with a more experienced advisor? If, so, where and when?

I did not have an opportunity to intern.

What advice would you give an undergrad student who was considering financial services/planning as a career?

This is a great career for many. If you want to pursue it, go for it! Research the many ways in which you can participate in this profession. Seek out mentors. Commit to lifelong learning. Know that at times it will be far from easy, but worth it. Always remember it is an honor and privilege to be entrusted with such an important part of a someone's life. Serve them well.

Do you think the average consumer is confused by all of the labels advisors use? Do you think the industry should restrict the use of "titles"?

In my experience, I have witnessed consumers be more misled than outwardly confused. I think when professionals present themselves to consumers as "financial advisors", it leads consumers to trust and believe that they are qualified to address all of their financial concerns, when that may or may not be the case. The financial services landscape is extremely complex, from offering appropriate advice to identifying products and strategies that best address clients' needs, all while understanding and educating the client on how decisions in one area may impact others. I believe professionals at all levels have significant value to offer their clients. I also believe consumers deserve a simplistic way of being able to quickly understand the degree to which a professional can competently address their needs.

Elaborate on your niche. What is it? Why this group? What skillsets are necessary to work with this group? Would you take the same approach if you had to start over?

I would define my niche as preparing African American, women professionals and business owners for life after full-time work or retirement. I focus intently on this group because I have spent my entire life around Black women who work extremely hard for so many people – children, spouses, employers, businesses, aging parents – for most of their adult lives; yet, who often enter into what can be the most vulnerable years of their own lives ill-prepared to live well. I want to change this. The skillsets I bring to working with this group are both qualitative and technical. First and foremost, I desire to prepare my clients for high-quality longevity. I encourage them to strive for a long, healthy life – physically, mentally, emotionally, and financially. My clients find me relatable and empathetic to the challenges they face in achieving optimal health on all fronts. I also bring strong technical skills in the areas of accumulating, structuring, and protecting wealth sufficient to fund longevity, as well as the skillset necessary to decumulate assets through creating an efficient retirement income stream.

I would take the same approach if I had to start over. I feel purposed in both, my work and who I serve.

If you could take a "mulligan" on your career, what would you do differently?

If could take a "mulligan" the one thing I would do differently would be to take the leap sooner. I spent a lot of years in roles that were important, but ancillary to providing advisory services. Ironically, I grew up professionally in Atlanta. It may be surprising for people to learn that despite being in a city like Atlanta and working in financial institutions with large footprints, I never encountered a single African American financial advisor and few women advisors. Fortunately, things have changed; but, not seeing advisors who looked like me made being out front, leading a financial advisory practice feel out of reach. This experience helps fuel my passion to serve in the way that I do. Just as I did not encounter advisors who looked like me, I also rarely encountered clients who did. So, in retrospect, I would just jump.

Mark Haywood

Professional Biography

- S. Mark Haywood II
- Educational Background
  - BA Economics, Cornell University, NY
  - BA Africana Studies, Cornell University, NY
  - MS Finance, University of Houston, TX
  - MA Biblical Studies, Grace School of Theology, TX
- Financial Advisor since August 2012
- Series 6, Series 63, Series 7

- MDRT Qualifier since 2013
- Social Media Links, Articles, Interviews
    - http://www.mark-haywood.com/
    - How to Invest During COVID-19 | Martha Stewart
    - Real Talk About Commission-Based Careers
    - A Mutual Selection Process

Why did you choose this field?

I selected this field because I truly love working with people, and I truly love making an impact. After graduating from Cornell, found myself in this interesting space where I maintained an interest in field of finance, but was unsure of what direction to go. I knew that I didn't want to do traditional economics, I was uninspired by traditional banking, and I definitely didn't want the lifestyle grind of investment banking. So, while I navigated the field of corporate finance, I found myself presented with the opportunity to explore personal financial planning. Ultimately, I chose this field because it provided the opportunity to have the best of all worlds: serving others, while maintaining a healthy work-life balance.

What experience caused you to consider leaving the field? What made you stay?

I've never considered leaving the field of personal finance. I've seen too many life-changing effects (upon clients and advisors alike) to ever have that be a thought. However, there were two moments that truly gave me conviction to stick it out no matter what. Both entailed helping these families navigate their financial planning in the aftermath of personal tragedies. I found myself inspired by each family's resilience, and I found myself honored to serve them in their time of need. Those instances emboldened me to view this profession as a higher calling, to fight through any personal challenges, and to put "self" aside in order to serve, love, and care for others.

What would you consider the "standard" for our industry?

The "STANDARD" for our industry has changed over the course of time. I would say presently the standard is to develop an integrated practice that involves both insurance and investments, operating in a comprehensive and cohesive manner.

I'm not sure how to answer this question. However, I would say that one lingering perception by consumers is that we are a commodity-driven industry. They view us as salespeople hocking insurance or securities, rather than integrated planners. Thus, their pursuit is less about integrated value and comprehensive planning, and more about maximum benefit for minimal cost and highest discount.

Approximately what percentage of your clients are Black? Is this by choice or default?

80-85% of my client-base is Black... both by choice and by default. The lack of joint-work opportunities is the main roadblock in acquiring clients of other demographics. I have noticed that my White counterparts tend to approach me to collaborate on cases with almost exclusively Black prospects. While it may not be intentional, it speaks to an inherent bias that I am often out-of-sight-and-out-of-mind… until a black person is in-their-sight-and-in-their mind.

By sheer statistics, demographics, and math… acquiring clients of other races would increase my overall wealth.

What roadblocks have you had acquiring clients of other races?

Black Financial Service Professionals are hindered in their pursuit of wealth by nothing more than the scope of their network. Opportunities are found not simply in WHAT we know (because we are some of the most educated and credentialed advisors by demographic), but by WHO we know. The more chances we have to connect with venture capitalists, politicians, C-suite executives, and power brokers will translate into opportunities to invest with, partner with, and build wealth those individuals. Unfortunately, a lot of those aforementioned individuals are not Black, and often we lack the avenues to connect with those individuals who operate in typically Non-Black spaces.

If you were not able to acquire clients of other races, what impact do you think it would have on your overall wealth?

No, generational wealth transfer isn't in jeopardy by not acquiring clients of other races. "Jeopardy" implies "will not happen." Black people are too resilient and creative for "will not happen." When doors close, we find new doors, or build our own. So, when it comes to generational wealth transfer… we may be slowed, and it may take longer, but we cannot (and will not) be stopped. And, we, especially, will not by stopped lack of non-Black clients.

Are Black Financial Services Professionals hindered in their pursuit of building wealth? If so, what are the factors that impact it?

Incentives to increase Black advisors:

- Internships & Co-Ops
- Work-Study programs
- Mentorship Programs

Were you given an opportunity to intern with a more experienced advisor? If, so, where and when?

Yes. My first four months in the business, I had the opportunity to be mentored two gentlemen (both white) in my network office. They took me under their wing and apprenticed me through joint-work, so that I could truly learn and understand the sales cycle, as well as client relations. I was fortunate in that they tremendously helped me learn the nuances of the business faster, and get up to speed quicker.

What advice would you give an undergrad student who was considering financial services/planning as a career?

Advice to an undergrad considering this career: Bet on yourself, trust in your ability, and don't take "no" as a final answer.

Elaborate on your niche. What is it? Why this group? What skillsets are necessary to work with this group?

I work exceptionally well with consultants, whether with big firm employees or independent business owners. The greatest skillset one can have working with these individuals is adaptability. To understand the need for adaptability, one must understand the "peaks and valleys" nature of the consulting profession. Consultants tend to have very transient lives, often moving from city-to-city and coast-to-coast for their next project or job opportunity. They tend to be highly compensated, but that compensation often comes in the form of bonuses, stock, and stock options. Their compensation also tends to come in large tranches, rather than a simple flow of recurring income and/or salary. Therefore, an advisor must be nimble and adept at creating a plan that provides the utmost of flexibility for their clients, and be ready to service that client's unique needs at any given moment.

Do you think the average consumer is confused by all of the labels advisors use? Do you think the industry should restrict the use of "titles"?

The average consumer is absolutely confused by all of the labels advisors use. Most consumers value competence far more than they value titles and certifications. However, consumers still value those titles and certifications to an extent because of their inherently "perceived" credibility (hence why we call it "credentialing"). So while the industry should not restrict the use of titles, it may be helpful to find ways to find ways to simplify and stream line those titles.

Would you take the same approach if you had to start over?

I would take the exact same approach if I had to start over. The fundamentals of this business never change: dial the phone, go see people, and get referrals so that you can dial the phone and see more people.

If you could take a "mulligan" on your career, what would you do differently?

If I could take a mulligan on my career, I would've more quickly developed an "abundance" mindset over a "scarcity" mindset. It took me too long to understand that not every client is a good client. Early in my career, during the "feast or famine" years, I held onto some client relationships where the interaction was toxic, the demands were beyond the scope of my work, or the margins were simply unprofitable. In the financial services business, you must understand your value proposition and know that every client isn't a good fit for your practice. However, you must also have the confidence to know that as you prune prospects and clients that are a poor fit, your selectivity makes room for those who are a good fit. There are no shortage of clients who need what you do, and want to work with you. And, conversely, passing on the clients that are not a good fit allows those clients the freedom to connect with other advisors who are a good fit. That's the "abundance" mindset – everyone can win.

Intentionally Left Blank

Roxanne Jones

Professional Biography

Roxanne M. Jones is a native of Los Angeles, California. She earned her Bachelor of Science Degree in Engineering at California State University, Northridge. Fortunately, she never professionally entered the Engineering field, as God had other plans for this outgoing, people-loving woman. She entered the Financial Services industry over 27 years ago and has never looked back. One who loves to learn and makes herself a resource for others, she returned to school to pursue an MBA and earned her degree at Pepperdine University.

She brings over 27 years of experience to the Financial Services industry, working for firms such as AIG Advisor Group, National Planning Corporation, and Securities Service Network. She is currently a Financial Advisor with

Independent Capital Management/SagePoint Financial, Inc, specializing in overall wealth management. She educates clients with respect to retirement, college, investment, and insurance planning in addition to estate planning.

Roxanne continues to serve her community as a member of Spirit Filled Family Church in Hesperia, CA. She is a lifetime member of Delta Sigma Theta Sorority, Inc. and a member of the Inland Valley Alumnae Chapter. She has been an Adjunct Faculty member at West Los Angeles College, teaching Personal Finance. She was a founding board member of the Black Alumni Association at CSUN and the 2015 recipient of their Volunteer Service Award. She has served on the National and Regional Boards for the National Society of Black Engineers. Currently she sits on the board for Camille Russell Wooden Ministries and Know Leadership, which educates at-risk students about college.

Most recently she has completed the dfree Inaugural Class and Leadership Training. Dfree is a financial literacy course designed to educate on the subject of being free from debt, delinquencies, and deficits and having deposits, deeds, and dividends. As a Leader she plans to work with churches and organizations to continue her purpose of helping others achieve financial freedom.

Roxanne enjoys helping others find the purpose and destiny God has for their lives. Her passion is to help others and she strives daily to do just that.

Why did you choose this field?

Interestingly enough, I didn't choose this field, it chose me. I had finished college with an Engineering degree and searched high and low for a position. My goal in life at that time was to teach and train new employees, so I began looking for Management Training positions. I interviewed with Independent Capital Management, my first group interview, and was told I could run and manage my own office anywhere I desired with the support of the company and that I could do it within two to three years; perfect for me. The next step was just passing exams and completing a training program. In my naivety, I still didn't even realize it was sales until I began that training. The goal of the position was educating people about their finances and teaching them how to utilize various investment vehicles to achieve their financial goals and dreams. It made sense to me and I both saw and felt the importance of that information. So, I hit the ground running and never turned back.

What experience caused you to consider leaving the field? What made you stay?

The only thing that ever made me consider leaving the field is earnings. The fluctuation in income would challenge me at times, but ultimately, I enjoy the fact that I am in charge. In this field, I am the only one who can stand in the way of earning what wages I want.

What made me stay?

Every time I would think, oh I'll just get a salaried position, my clients would call with assets to move or I would get referral calls, and business would start to move again. I would think about my clients and ask myself, "Who will take care of them?" This would always motivate me to continue.

What would you consider the "standard" for our industry?

Financial advisors that offer total wealth management. They should be licensed in securities (stocks, bonds, mutual funds, alternative investments) and insurance; and have the ability, resources, or partnerships to offer real estate as well as estate planning. Services should include review of spending habits, retirement, investment and college planning as well as insurance needs.

Our industry is moving more towards fee-based planning versus commission or a balance of both.

What do you perceive the consumer sees as the "standard"?

Consumers seek Certified Financial Planners. Many people that I've encountered don't know the difference, they just want someone to help them with their finances.

Approximately what percentage of your clients are Black? Is this by choice or default?

90 – 95%, this is by choice and default. I started in the business with my friends and branched to their parents, grandparents and ultimately referrals which were all primarily Black. The non-Black clients I have came through home shows or referrals. I will work with anyone, but the need in the Black community is great due to the nature of our spending habits and lack of knowledge about financial planning, so our community is always a focus.

What roadblocks have you had acquiring clients of other races?

Since I've built my practice primarily through referrals, having majority Black clients has meant that the majority of my new clients are also Black. Another roadblock has been my own lack of networking in other communities – I enjoy working with and supporting the Black community, and so I haven't focused on outreach.

If you were not able to acquire clients of other races, what impact do you think it would have on your overall wealth?

Over my years in the business, I have experienced not generating income due to lack of client diversity in my practice. In comparison to other colleagues and their practice, there is a difference in my overall profit. As a result, I have to acquire more clients than some of my colleagues to generate equal income.

Are Black Financial Services Professionals hindered in their pursuit of building wealth? If so, what are the factors that impact it?

No, I don't believe Black Financial Services Professionals are hindered in their pursuit of building wealth. Our industry is necessary for every individual. The opportunity for building wealth is vast, but it requires discipline, drive, and consistency.

Is the generational wealth transfer of Black Financial Services Professionals in jeopardy due to an inability to acquire clients of other races?

In part. The inability to acquire clients of other races definitely hampers generational wealth transfer, because you are forced to rely on a minority population within a larger, national population. Acquiring clients of other races gives you access to a larger portion of the public, and builds a steadier foundation for when business slows down, as you have more clients to rely on.

The American College for Financial Services has a scholarship targeted towards African-Americans to increase the numbers of us in the field. What other incentives do you think our industry can put in place to achieve this goal?

Internships and/or mentoring programs to bring exposure to the industry and the various directions one could take.

Were you given an opportunity to intern with a more experienced advisor? If so, where and when?

Yes, our company provides a training program to prepare you for going into the field. Each representative works with someone that guides them through the program, does weekly check-ins, and aids in preparation and debriefing of appointments.

What advice would you give an undergrad student who was considering financial services/planning as a career?

I would make sure they had an understanding that this is their own business. What you put into growing your business will determine its success. If they aren't driven, I would encourage them to look at other opportunities within the industry.

Elaborate on your niche. What is it? Why this group? What skill sets are necessary to work with this group?

My niche is overall wealth management. Being in the business for 27 years now and still maintaining roughly 80%

of my original clients from those first three years in the business, my niche has been determined by my clients' needs. They define my target market, which is professionals, aged 45 to 70, mid to upper income, homeowners, with children. Wealth management is their top priority, as they focus on retirement, college funds, investments and insurance while creating a financial legacy for their children.

Working with this group requires me to have a broad knowledge of everything – wealth management may be my focus, but I have to keep abreast of any and all changes in products and opportunities. To that end I am always focused on learning about what else I can provide for my clients to advance their goals. I have yet to segment my clientele and focus in just one or two areas.

Do you think the average consumer is confused by all of the label's advisors use? Do you think the industry should restrict the use of "titles"?

Yes, realtors, insurance agents, accountants, tax preparers and credit repair all hold themselves as Financial Professionals, all use separate and distinct jargon, and all offer different services.

I do believe titles should be restricted and industry regulated. At my Broker/Dealer only 65/66 licensed at can use the title Financial Advisor/Planner otherwise they are Financial Services Professionals.

Would you take the same approach if you had to start over?

I would take largely the same approach, as I have been successful at building a practice through referrals and enjoy my client base, but given the chance, I would have added to that by attending networking events to bring diversity in my clients earlier in my career.

If you could take a "mulligan" on your career, what would you do differently?

- I would have not changed broker/dealers four times.
- I would have acquired more asset under management before going into a management position.
- I would have diversified my clientele.

JL Wilson

Professional Biography

- ✓ Educational background B.S. (Tuskegee M.E.) MBA (Loyola New Orleans focus on entrepreneurship
- ✓ Years in the industry (34 years)
- ✓ Licenses, professional certifications or designations (Life, Series 6/63, CLU®, CLTC®, Lifetime MDRT)

Why did you choose this field?

When I was a junior in college my father died and the family only had a $500 death policy on him. That situation bothered me and it made me want to "help my people" avoid that type of situation. When I was looking to change occupations, I interviewed with NY Life because I was still determined to help our people. Our Managing Partner at the time was Cassius Williams, Sr. (the first Black to hold that position at NY Life) showed me how I would make significantly more money than being an engineer. Since then, I have been a resource to my community in the areas of financial planning and insurance.

What experience caused you to consider leaving the field?

I had difficulty in getting people to "do the right thing" in terms of preparing for their financial future and that created problems with respect to me paying my bills. Most of the prospects that I encountered were reluctant to do the proper planning

What made you stay?

In comparing my income when 2 people "did the right thing" compared to a 40–50-hour job, I knew that I was in the right industry.

What would you consider the "standard" for our industry?

Designations are a good thing without question [Note: I have several], but financial professionals can be successful without them. As I see it, the "standard" is hitting personal goals/targets and helping the people you support in your target market.

What do you perceive the consumer sees as the "standard"?

I used to think it was all of the initials behind your name, and that may still be the case, but I am too far removed from getting more at this point (i.e. not going back to school). Most that I've encountered recognize the benchmark of MDRT (which I have lifetime status).

Approximately what percentage of your clients are Black? 90-95%. Is this by choice or default?

By default, but was my goal when getting into the business was helping my people, and that led me to more and more of my people. So, I will say by default, but as a subconscious design.

What roadblocks have you had acquiring clients of other races?

I didn't go after them that aggressively. When they came my way, I worked with them and asked for referrals. The ones that I do have (multiple ethnicities) love me and give referrals.

If you were not able to acquire clients of other races, what impact do you think it would have on your overall wealth?

My goal was never to be a billionaire, but I always wanted to make more money. The economic make-up of my clientele could be impacting my wealth.

Are Black Financial Services Professionals hindered in their pursuit of building wealth?

I don't think so. The current generation (Millennials) are looking more towards black professionals.

Is the generational wealth transfer of Black Financial Services Professionals in jeopardy due to an inability to acquire clients of other races?

It would be helpful if I had more to transfer; however, I have been able to offset that by buying more life insurance in order to transfer the amount that I had in mind since I may not have "earned" it.

The American College for Financial Services has a scholarship targeted towards African-Americans to increase the numbers of us in the field. What other incentives do you think our industry can put in place to achieve this goal?

Social media marketing campaigns targeted to the Minority community (like the restaurant chains do). Cell phones provide immediate info.

You could get the attention of your by creating a video game for exposure to these critical topics

Were you given an opportunity to intern with a more experienced advisor?

No

If, so, where and when?

I came straight into NYLife and my Managing Partner encouraged me to utilize the resources here when I showed initiative.

What advice would you give an undergrad student who was considering financial services/planning as a career?

Internships!!!!

Do you think the average consumer is confused by all of the labels advisors use?

Yes.

Do you think the industry should restrict the use of "titles"?

Yes, so the consumer knows what they are getting and paying for.

Elaborate on your niche. What is it?

Employee benefits.

Why this group?

It allowed me to create residual revenue to offset the lack of income generated from individual clients. African-Americans (Blue/White collar) needed my guidance more than anyone else.

What skillsets are necessary to work with this group?

Understanding product/market and how to communicate. It is important to speak in layperson terms and not industry Jargon.

Would you take the same approach if you had to start over?

Hindsight is 20/20. My goal when coming to NYLife was to be a CFP, but NYLife didn't have it at the time. Cassius (our Managing Partner) directed me to group benefits to get my foot in the door. The CFP was all but abandoned until NYLife's "Eagle Strategies" Program came along.

If you could take a "mulligan" on your career, what would you do differently?

I would have stayed the course of a CFP, even if I had to go to a different company to do so. Don't let people take your dreams away.

References

US Bureau of Labor Statistics. 2019. *Labor Force Statistics from the Current Population Survey.* [online] Available at: <https: bus.gov/PCs/demographics.htm>

Hunt, V., Dixon-Fyle, S., Prince, S. and Dolan, K., 2020. *Diversity wins: How inclusion matters.* [online] McKinsey & Company. Available at: <https://www.mckinsey.com/~/media/mckinsey/featured%20insights/diversity%20and%20inclusion/diversity%20wins%20how%20inclusion%20matters/diversity-wins-how-inclusion-matters-vf.pdf> [Accessed 18 June 2021].

Herring, Cedric. "Does Diversity Pay?". *American Sociological Review*, 2009, https://www.asanet.org/sites/default/files/savvy/images/journals/docs/pdf/asr/Apr09ASRFeature.pdf. Accessed 19 June 2021.

Fry, Richard. "Millennials Overtake Baby Boomers As America's Largest Generation". *Pew Research Center*, 2020, https://www.pewresearch.org/fact-tank/2020/04/28/millennials-overtake-baby-boomers-as-americas-largest-generation/. Accessed 19 June 2020.

Hewlett, Sylvia Ann et al. "How Diversity Can Drive Innovation". *Harvard Business Review*, 2013, https://hbr.org/2013/12/how-diversity-can-drive-innovation. Accessed 19 June 2021.

Moten, & Rauch. Introductory Financial Management: Theory and Application. BVT Publishing 2017, https://www.bvtpublishing.com/book/1028

Made in the USA
Monee, IL
03 November 2026

67384996R00075